Fylling's Illustrated Guide to

NATURE IN YOUR NEIGHBORHOOD

Marni Fylling

Heyday, Berkeley, California

Copyright © 2020 by Marni Fylling

Library of Congress Cataloging-in-Publication Data

Names: Fylling, Marni, author.
Title: Fylling's illustrated guide to nature in your neighborhood / Marni Fylling.
Description: Berkeley, California : Heyday, [2020] | Includes bibliographical references.
Identifiers: LCCN 2019047612 | ISBN 9781597144803 (paperback)
Subjects: LCSH: Natural history--United States.
Classification: LCC QH104 .F95 2020 | DDC 508.73--dc23
LC record available at https://lccn.loc.gov/2019047612
Cover Art: Marni Fylling
Cover Design: Ashley Ingram
Interior Design/Typesetting: Ashley Ingram

Published by Heyday
P.O. Box 9145, Berkeley, California 94709
(510) 549-3564
heydaybooks.com

Printed in Korea by Four Colour Print Group, Louisville, Kentucky

10 9 8 7 6 5 4 3 2 1

CONTENTS

For Cathy and Kimi, my fellow adventurers,
and Mom, Dad, Marilyn, and Rowan, with love.

ACKNOWLEDGMENTS

So many people helped make this book possible, and that was part of the fun—learning what friends and family find in their neighborhoods, reconnecting with colleagues from my past, and contacting perfect strangers who were so generous with their time and expertise. Victoria Schlesinger came up with the idea in an impromptu brainstorming session, and I couldn't wait to research our often overlooked and misunderstood urban flora and fauna.

The excellent and enthusiastic bunch at Heyday put everything together beautifully, as always. Many thanks to Ashley, Marthine, Briony, Diane, Christopher, Mariko, and Gayle.

Chris Giorni helped tremendously with the species list and the reptile and amphibian chapters; Art Shapiro narrowed down the lepidopteran lineup; Andre and Keriann Fylling, Brian Ort, Camille Hill, and Rachael Suczek sent their valuable observations; John Kuo, Rob Longair, and Kerry Barringer reviewed chapters and patiently answered many, many emails on details; Patricia T. O'Connor, Stewart Kellerman, Kevin Rice, Lucia Jacobs, Elina Lastro Nino, Lynn Kimsey, and Gabrielle Nevitt graciously responded to my nitpicky queries. All remaining errors are mine.

I couldn't have done the illustrations without these amazing naturalists, who are also talented photographers: John Welch, Rob Longair, Zachary Lim, and Jacqueline Sones (from her wonderful bodegahead.blogspot.com). Mick scanned every illustration *again*, and Rowan relinquished the computer when I really needed it.

All my dear friends and family, and the Little City Books crew, provided so much love and support throughout. I am honored and grateful to have you in my life. Thank you!!

INTRODUCTION

My love of nature began in our tiny backyard in downtown Sacramento, California. With no forests, streams, or trails, my sister, best friend, and I still managed to find a world of wonder and delight among the weeds and grass around us. We rescued worms from sidewalks, examined snails' tentacles, and munched on Sourgrass. Countless caterpillars, ladybugs, and pillbugs were given tender, moss-lined homes in peanut butter jars and our trusty plastic Easter baskets. We learned what they ate by trial and error, and watched their fascinating life cycles taking place before our eyes.

It's easy to assume that you have to travel to find nature, but there is more outside your door than you might realize. Each plant and animal in your neighborhood, as ordinary as it may seem, is beautifully adapted to its life near humans—and may hold a surprise or two. Did you know that poison oak and poison ivy are related to mangoes? That House Finches were once smuggled across the country? Or that mice sing?

Most of the little marvels I treasured as a child were not native to California. Unlike species in the wilderness, many urban flora and fauna were introduced by people, either intentionally (as pets, food, medicine, or a reminder of faraway homes) or unintentionally (in soil, in food, or attached to livestock or clothing.) Introduced species sometimes thrive in their new land; with no natural predators or diseases, they may displace the native inhabitants.

Even if we are now more aware of the impact we have on nature, we still have a huge influence on the wildlife surrounding us. All living things need food, water, and shelter. Our homes are permanent, temperature-controlled structures with a reliable source of water, and we load up on anything we want to eat at the grocery store. Wild plants and animals, exposed to the elements and seasons, must change their room and board accordingly. Our houses and yards provide a welcome bounty of warmth, shelter, food, and water for creatures in the city, especially in the lean autumn and winter months. If we get to know the animals and plants around us, we can be better neighbors.

Keep in mind that wild animals are not on the prowl for people—most would like nothing more than to be left alone. If frightened or threatened, they understandably try to protect themselves and may bite or scratch. Be cautious and respectful, but don't be afraid. Quietly observe birds and mammals from afar, or use a pair of binoculars to better appreciate their patterns and behavior.

A NOTE ON NAMING

Common names seem simple, but can be confusing: in different regions, the same plant or animal can have different names—the plant known as purslane is also called duckweed, pigweed, red root, and pursley, among other things. To make matters worse, the same common name may grace multiple species—"pigweed" can refer to a wide array of plants that pigs feast upon.

Scientific names found alongside the illustrations in this

book (and in the appendix) are specific to each creature or plant. A scientific name, or binomial, has two parts, the genus and the species, usually derived from Greek or Latin. Western Poison Oak is *Toxicodendron diversilobum*. The genus name, *Toxicodendron*, means "poison tree" in Greek; the species name, *diversilobum*, or "diverse lobes," refers to its astonishing variety of leaf shapes. For clarity, a common name that denotes a particular species will be capitalized; if it can be used to refer to multiple species, the name will not be capitalized—for example, "The *Eastern Gray Squirrel* is one of many types of North American *tree squirrel*."

This slim volume is an introduction to a selection of the most commonly seen urban and suburban plants and animals. Many occur throughout the United States; where similar species exist, a western example is shown—for instance, while there are dozens of garter snakes species in the United States, this book highlights the Western Garter Snake. If you find yourself particularly interested in a group of plants or animals, dive into a comprehensive field guide, where you will find descriptions of all the members of that group, or all the wildlife specific to your locale.

TIME TO GO OUTSIDE!

There was great joy and comfort to be found in my childhood slice of nature, and humble as it was, it inspired a lifelong interest in science and the environment. Significant and wide-ranging benefits can be gained from spending time outside: nature stimulates all of our senses—it can reduce stress and fatigue, improve concentration and clarity, and boost mental health.

Nature is all around us! Put away your cell phone, walk outside, and take a look. If you don't have a yard, explore a local park or even the cracks in the sidewalk. Immerse yourself in the ecosystem of a grassy lawn, a weed and its inhabitants, or the microcosm of a single flower. See what you discover! Refresh and expand your world by learning something new about a plant or animal you've been familiar with your whole life.

PLANTS

Pint-sized or sprawling, most backyards share a common element—green! The very thing that makes a garden green (the pigment chlorophyll) is what makes life on earth possible. Through photosynthesis, plants use chlorophyll to capture energy from the sun and convert carbon dioxide and water into oxygen, which we breathe, and into sugars, which sustain animals and humans alike. Imagine if you could just stand in the sun for nourishment (eating is kind of fun, though).

Plants (like all living things) need strategies for survival, dispersal, and reproduction, but face the extra challenge of being rooted to one spot. Some reproduce asexually, growing stems across soil or underground to sprout identical clones that won't offer competition for space and sunlight. Flowers are agents of sexual reproduction (which creates genetic diversity), containing either an egg inside a pistil, fertilizing pollen on anthers, or both. Successful pollination results in a seed within a fruit; anything with seeds (tomato, cucumber, even a pod of peas!) is a fruit.

Grasses and many trees are wind-pollinated, producing legions of pollen that fill the air (and tickle our noses), in hopes of landing on the pistils of other flowers. Most flowering plants employ a more reliable method of reproduction and so need much less pollen: they entice animal pollinators with a meal of sweet nectar and/or protein-rich pollen. Their pollen travels to other flowers, dusted on hummingbirds' foreheads, or on the legs of bees, butterflies, or beetles.

The most impressive plant treks are often undertaken by seeds: catapulting, wafting through the air, or hitching a ride on (or inside) an animal, seeds get around! Human migrations have extended the range of these trips—colonists traveling to America had carefully packed seeds from their homelands to use as food or medicine; many stowaways also made the voyage, in wool and soil and on clothing.

Any plant growing where a human doesn't want it is called a weed, whether native to the area or not. Since weedy species are common across different regions and are also among the most misunderstood plants, this chapter will concentrate on them. These persistent plants are talented survivalists, often able to grow in incredibly hostile conditions with little water, soil, or space. They may be tough to get rid of, but it's difficult not to admire their grit and tenacity.

Many of these weeds have edible portions, but don't partake unless you can identify them with absolute certainty. Also keep in mind that plants absorb pollutants—stay away from anything growing near a busy road or in an area that might be contaminated with pesticides or other chemicals.

COMMON DAISY
(flower to 1 ¼ inches wide)

It's hard to imagine a more cheerful flower than the Common Daisy (*Bellis perennis*); making crowns and necklaces of daisy chains is a lazy-summer-day tradition. The genus name means "pretty," and "daisy" comes from "day's eye"—as the petals (which close at night) open to greet the morning. This winking habit is common to many flowers, perhaps to protect their reproductive parts from the elements or nighttime predators. Native to Europe, the perennial flowers have become naturalized in most parts of the world, their low-growing rosette of leaves blending right into the lawn.

Like a dandelion, cosmos, or sunflower, a single daisy is not single at all; it's composed of many flowers. Each white, often pink-tipped "petal" is a ray flower; each little yellow bump in the daisy's center is a disk flower. A wonderful strategy, really: the bright ray flowers attract pollinators, and each visit pollinates multiple flowers. Think of how many sunflower seeds are produced in one sunflower, and you can see the potential!

COMMON DANDELION
(flower to 2 inches wide)

Children delight in dandelions—radiant yellow blooms are followed by fabulous balls of plumed seeds that fly into the air and grant wishes with a single puff. Most adults are far less smitten with this common and tenacious weed. With a perennial and low-growing, mostly underground stem, a taproot up to three feet deep, and flowers (all ray flowers) that produce up to two hundred airborne seeds each, it's almost impossible to eradicate from the garden.

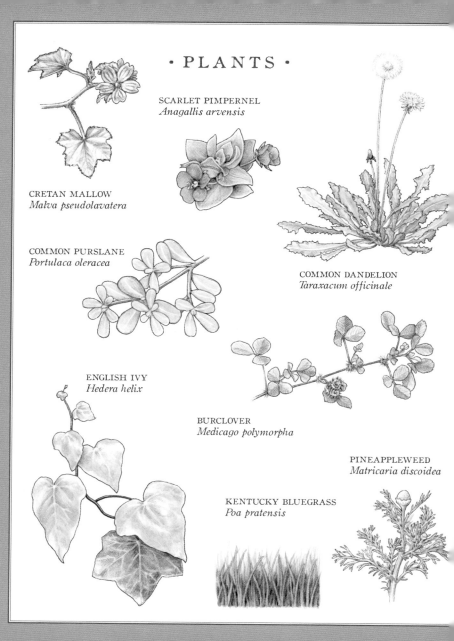

· PLANTS ·

CRETAN MALLOW
Malva pseudolavatera

SCARLET PIMPERNEL
Anagallis arvensis

COMMON PURSLANE
Portulaca oleracea

COMMON DANDELION
Taraxacum officinale

ENGLISH IVY
Hedera helix

BURCLOVER
Medicago polymorpha

PINEAPPLEWEED
Matricaria discoidea

KENTUCKY BLUEGRASS
Poa pratensis

EASTERN POISON IVY
Toxicodendron radicans

WESTERN POISON OAK
Toxicodendron diversilobum

FOXTAIL
Hordeum sp.
spikelet and spike

COMMON STORKSBILL
Erodium cicutarium
seed, fruit, and plant

BERMUDA BUTTERCUP
Oxalis pes-caprae

ENGLISH PLANTAIN
Plantago lanceolata

COMMON DAISY
Bellis perennis

Our relationship with dandelions wasn't always antagonistic. European settlers first brought Common Dandelions to North America as a valuable food and medicine. One of the first greens to appear in early spring, its leaves, flowers, and roots are quite nutritious (dandelion wine, whole flower tempura, or dandelion salad, anyone?). The scientific name, *Taraxacum officinale*, derived from the Greek words for "disorder" and "remedy," refers to its curative powers. Other animals also enjoy the bounty—gophers dig the roots, insects sip its nectar, and birds feast on the seeds.

The name dandelion has its origin in the French *dent de lion*, or "lion's tooth," likely from the jagged-edged leaves.

ENGLISH PLANTAIN
(leaves 3–12 inches long)

Common in lawns and disturbed areas, English Plantain grows as a rosette. Each distinctive narrow leaf bears three to five lengthwise ribs. Out of the center rise tall, thin stalks, each topped with an oval cluster of tiny flowers. Opening in stages, from bottom to top, the flowers form an advancing ring of yellowish-white anthers on slender filaments, like a fancy brim on a tiny hat.

Some populations of English Plantain self-fertilize; others are mostly wind-pollinated, the pollen sometimes contributing to hay fever. Buckeye butterflies (page 47) lay their eggs on the leaves. Rabbits and gophers nosh on their tasty leaves, and birds, mice, and insects eat the small brown seeds.

Sun-loving English Plantains are fairly drought tolerant, and are related to the Broadleaf Plantain, which has shorter, wider leaves and a longer, narrower flowering spike.

COMMON STORKSBILL
(flower to ½ inch wide)

The lovely rosy-lavender flowers of Common Storksbill (also called filaree) are little geraniums, in the same family as the cultivated garden staple. While it provides pollen, nectar, and forage for a number of animals, its most fascinating features make it a difficult weed. The elongate stork-bill-shaped fruit (sometimes playfully fashioned into "scissors") bursts open when ripe, launching five seeds into the air. And they are not your run-of-the-mill seeds— they plant themselves! Each sharp-tipped seed has a long corkscrew attachment that straightens when wet, and coils tightly as it dries. Combined with backward-pointing hairs on the seed and tail, this action bores the seed into the soil—or into socks or pet fur. Spiraling or unwinding only takes a few minutes—it's worth tossing a seed or two into water to watch.

MALLOW
(flower to 1¼ inch wide)

This common weed is also called cheeseweed—the fruit resembles a diminutive wheel of (green) cheese. Plants spread quickly and can grow well over two feet tall with hairy, lobed leaves borne on woody stems, and delicate white to pale pink flowers that bloom most of the year. A deep taproot makes this annual drought resistant.

Mallows are related to cotton, hibiscus, Okra, and the plant originally used to make marshmallows (the mucilaginous thickener made from its roots has since been replaced with gelatin). Most parts are edible, but not particularly tasty, and they can accumulate toxins from fertilizers.

BURCLOVER
(flower to ⅜ inch wide)

With bundles of dainty yellow flowers and clover leaflets in groups of three, this trailing plant looks innocent enough until it becomes covered with what appear to be little green sea urchins! Look closely to appreciate the spiral design of these spiny fruits. They turn brown and hard as they dry, easily clinging to clothes or fur to get a free ride for dispersing minute, kidney-bean-shaped seeds. Like some fellow members of the pea family, Burclover's roots have a symbiotic relationship with a bacterium that converts nitrogen from the air into natural fertilizer—it is sometimes grown as a cover crop to increase the fertility of the soil.

Burclover is often a lawn pest—be careful walking barefoot or handling those prickly burs. Ouch!

BERMUDA BUTTERCUP
(flower to 1 ½ inches wide)

Bermuda Buttercup is not related to "true" buttercups, and it doesn't hail from Bermuda. Another name is Sourgrass, since the clusters of sunny yellow blooms, heart-shaped leaflets (arranged like shamrocks), and stems have a tart flavor. The sharpness comes from oxalic acid, fine for most people to eat in small quantities.

If you have Bermuda Buttercups, you probably have lots of them, even though they don't set seeds (only one of the two flower types necessary for fertilization is found in North America). Cheerful and delicate aboveground, the Bermuda Buttercup's underground activities help it prosper. Try to pull the plant up and you'll likely get only a handful of leaves; dig deeper, you might get a portion of the fragile underground stem; even deeper is the bulb the plant grew from, and below that is a translucent, carrot-like root that contracts to pull the underground stem (and the ten or more tear-shaped bulblets developing along it!) farther into, or along, the ground. Pieces of stem and the bulblets (which detach readily) give rise to new plants, so the weed is easily dispersed during planting and cultivation—which has allowed it to spread all over the world from its native South Africa.

Bermuda Buttercup bulblets may be the bane of human gardeners, but some birds and rodents eat them, and the flowers provide nectar for bees and butterflies.

Other common *Oxalis* species are more diminutive and may have pink or white blossoms, but all bear the same triad of clover-like leaves.

SCARLET PIMPERNEL

(flower to ½ inch wide)

These sweet flowers are petite but colorful—typically orange-red petals are occasionally bright blue or even white, and magenta stamens are tipped with yellow anthers. Closing in cloudy or cool weather, they are sometimes called Shepherd's Weatherglass.

If you examine the stem closely, you'll see that it's square in cross section. Also, look for the perfectly round, dangling fruit—when dried, the top opens like the lid of a cookie jar, releasing seeds to be carried off by rain or wind.

This low-growing annual is not edible, but it's appealing to the eye and not difficult to eradicate once it's taken root—you may choose to leave it in your garden to enjoy.

PINEAPPLEWEED
(flower to ⅜ inch wide)

Have you ever seen tiny shrubs full of miniature pineapples growing out of cracks in the sidewalk or around the edges of stepping stones? Actually more egg-shaped than pineapple-shaped, the flower heads and lacy leaves, when crushed, release a sweet pineappley scent reminiscent of chamomile (to which it's related). There are no ray flowers (petals), just between one hundred and five hundred greenish yellow disk flowers, so one plant can produce an extraordinary number of teensy seeds.

A hardy native of North America and Asia, Pineappleweed was introduced to Europe instead of vice versa. Able to grow in poor soil and dry, sunny conditions, this fragrant weed has been very successful in urban areas.

POISON OAK AND POISON IVY
(leaflet to 4 ½ inches long)

If it weren't for urushiol, the oily allergen found in all parts of poison oak and poison ivy plants (except the nectar and pollen), people would delight in these gorgeous plants. Lush, glossy, bright green, variably shaped leaflets grow in groups of three (occasionally five or even seven for poison oak)—two almost touching each other and the third on its own short stem. Cascades of tiny pale flowers give rise to white berries as the leaves change color in the autumn, yielding a spectacular display of purple, scarlet, pink, orange, and green. The plants can grow as shrubs, vines, or slim trees, and thrive in full sun and cool shade.

Alas, about 85 percent of people are sensitive to urushiol, which is easily transferred from poison oak's and poison ivy's leaves or stems to clothes, tools, or pets brushing by. This is not a problem for other animals: birds, mice, and squirrels feast on the berries and seeds; deer, horses, bears, and a number of insects have a taste for the leaves; and any number of small animals nest in or hide among the branches.

Species of poison oak are native to western and southwestern states; types of poison ivy occur in most states. Poison ivy's three leaflets are generally more pointed than the lobed leaves of poison oak. It's best to become familiar with these plants so you can avoid them—even bare winter stems can cause a rash. If you are exposed, wash with soap and plenty of cool water to avoid spreading the offending oil.

Poison oak, poison ivy, and poison sumac (in southeastern states) are part of the same plant family as pistachios, cashews, and mangoes. Urushiol is found in mango skin, not in the fruit below it; with cashews, removal of the shell and steaming or roasting destroys the toxin; when pistachios are harvested, the fleshy outer hull is stripped, and subsequent roasting takes care of residue on the shell.

ENGLISH IVY
(leaves to 4 inches long)

Associated with prestigious colleges and cozy cottages, where it provides elegance and insulation, this hardy, handsome evergreen is a quick-growing ground cover, sending out roots from an ever-lengthening stem. If it encounters a wall, tree, fence, or utility pole, English Ivy ascends: clusters of roots squeeze into nooks and crannies and produce a gluey substance to help it hold on tight.

Not sturdy enough to hold themselves upright, vines use a variety of climbing techniques to get closer to life-giving sunlight. Some grow in spirals around structures; others use curling, twining tendrils to gain a foothold. Boston Ivy, also common on walls and fences, is deciduous (it drops its leaves for winter). Unlike English Ivy, it employs branching tendrils with flattened, adhesive pads that do not penetrate the surface.

Native to Eurasia, English Ivy is popular because of its penchant for shady places, but its blankets of deep green can quickly envelop other plants and trees, blocking sunlight and eventually killing them. Stems exposed to full sun (usually at the top of a tree or high wall) produce "mature" diamond-shaped leaves and spherical bundles of greenish flowers. The flowers are a rich source of nectar, and the purple-black berries that result are fancied by a number of birds, who disperse the seeds. Don't snack on the berries yourself—most parts of English Ivy are somewhat poisonous.

COMMON PURSLANE
(flower to ⅜ inch wide)

The succulent, often red-edged leaves of Common Purslane are distinctive to this plant, loved for its culinary uses and loathed for its weedy properties. Purslane has been cultivated for centuries for its crisp, tangy leaves and is available at farmers' markets and restaurants all over the world. It's also likely to be in your yard, even in packed, dry soil. Left unchecked, the low-growing plant spreads out to form a dense mat, covered with yellow flowers—each flower matures into a petite lidded bowl, filled with teeny seeds. Over a season, a single plant can produce well over 200,000 seeds that may remain viable for years. Just by letting the plant be, you can enjoy unlimited access to tasty salad greens.

LAWN GRASSES
(6 inches to 3 feet tall)

Some of the first lawns (grass, clover, chamomile, et cetera, kept short) were maintained around medieval castles in France and Britain, yielding a clear view to protect against invasion; others were in the village commons, where sheep and cattle grazed. Public parks and sporting greens became popular in ensuing centuries, but since they had to be either grazed or cut by hand, private lawns remained signs of wealth. The advent of the mass-produced lawn mower in the 1890s finally made lawns accessible to homeowners in the growing suburbs.

Grass is a natural for a lawn. Unlike most other types of plants, which grow from their outermost tips, grass grows from its base, so it can be mowed, over and over, as long as it isn't cut too short. Bluegrasses and fescues are popular lawn grasses because they form sod: thick, emerald-green mats that discourage weed growth.

Have you ever wondered whether grass has flowers? Grass pollen is a common allergen, so it must come from somewhere! If grass isn't mowed, it grows a foot or more tall, and then sends up flowering stalks. The flowers last only a few days, and are no more than pistils and anther-bearing stamens hanging from small sheaths. Pollinated by the wind, grasses do not need to attract pollinators with colorful petals and syrupy nectar. Wheat, oats, rice, and other grains (grasses, it's true!) have been bred by humans for large, nutritious seeds. Most common lawn grasses produce tiny seeds that scatter on the breeze.

FOXTAIL

(2–3 feet tall)

While some grasses rely on wind for seed dispersal, a number of other grasses use a different strategy: silky, green, foxtail-shaped flowering spikes dry out and fall apart into barbed spikelets (also called foxtails) that cling to animal fur for seed dispersal. The problem is, with its pointed tip, backward-pointing hairs, and stiff, outward-pointing needlelike bristles, a foxtail lodges easily into an animal's face, paw, ear, or eye and relentlessly works its way in. Lay a foxtail flat on your palm, place your other hand on top, and rub your hand forward and backward a couple of times, and you'll see the foxtail moves in only one direction.

A foxtail is painful when it pokes into your shoes and socks, but embedded in a pet's skin, it can cause infection—and in extreme cases migrates through the body, leading to illness and even death.

Tender, green foxtail grass is tasty fodder for many animals; the seed inside each spikelet is also edible. Native Americans ground some species of foxtail seeds into a nutritious flour.

ANNELIDS

The annelids, or segmented worms, include scores of colorful characters from iridescent green beauties with golden swimming paddles to tube dwellers bearing plumes of fuchsia tentacles, and even pink burrowers with crowns of blood-red gills. There are predators, herbivores, filter feeders, scavengers, and parasites. The vast majority are marine. Some leech species live in freshwater; a few annelids are terrestrial, including the garden-variety earthworm.

EARTHWORM
(1–8 inches long)

Tender and defenseless, earthworms are packed with protein and almost universally appetizing in the animal kingdom. Streamlined, muscular bodies dig through soil with the help of small spines on each segment. These spines provide enough grip that a bird has to tug pretty hard to get a worm out of its burrow.

15

There are three types of earthworm: small red wigglers (like striped *Eisenia fetida*) live near the surface of the soil, feeding on leaf litter and manure, and are often used for composting; worms like the red-violet *Lumbricus rubellus* (frustratingly, they

are also called red wigglers) eat soil as they tunnel horizontally through the top layers; and large night crawlers (such as *Lumbricus*

terrestris) surface after dark, looking for leaves and other organic matter to drag into their deep, permanent, vertical burrows.

An earthworm does not drink water or have lungs—its thin skin must be kept moist to absorb water and oxygen. It emerges under cover of darkness on cool, damp nights to look for food, new habitat, or mates, and can safely travel farthest on rainy nights, since all surfaces are wet. If it wanders away from soil, it may get stranded (worms don't have much of a sense of direction) and die quickly from exposure or predation when

the sun comes up (but usually not from drowning—worms can survive in water if it contains enough oxygen, but will suffocate if their skin dries).

Earthworms are hermaphrodites—any two can exchange sperm, storing it until each worm is ready to lay eggs. The clitellum, a thickened section near the head end of a mature worm, secretes an elastic band that fills with eggs and sperm as the worm wriggles out. Then the ends seal shut, forming a little lemon-shaped cocoon.

Glaciers wiped out the worms in the northern United States during the Ice Age, and the native earthworms that live along the West Coast and in southeastern states are not found in disturbed habitats—you don't find them in areas populated by humans. Typical backyard worms are descendants of those brought by colonists with plants or ship ballast soil. Excellent for the garden (they mix and aerate soil and hasten decomposition, making nutrients available to plants), introduced earthworms are a menace in undeveloped areas, displacing native worms and threatening the northern forests that evolved without worms.

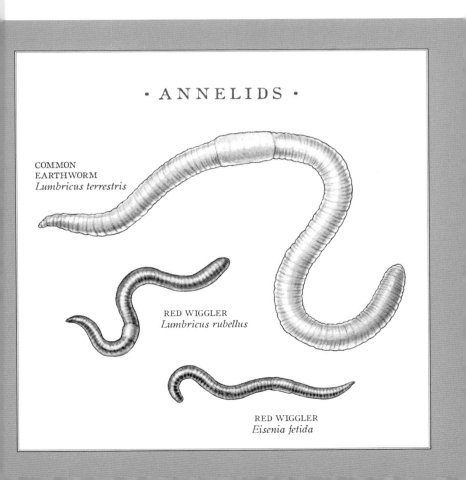

· ANNELIDS ·

COMMON
EARTHWORM
Lumbricus terrestris

RED WIGGLER
Lumbricus rubellus

RED WIGGLER
Eisenia fetida

MOLLUSKS

If you spot a snail or slug, spend a few minutes watching as it explores the world, waving its captivating retractable tentacles. Eyes peep out of the tips of the longer pair; the shorter pair points toward the ground. Seeking moist, shady places during the heat of the day and coming out at night or in wet weather, a snail or slug uses a ribbon of little rasping teeth to chow down on plants and anything it can scavenge.

Garden slugs and snails have lungs instead of gills, but are related to clams and octopuses, with similarly soft bodies prone to drying out. The solution? Mucus! Besides protecting their skin, it allows them to glide along on a muscular "foot," scaling walls and stems, and leaves a shimmering trail that contains useful information for other slugs and snails about their whereabouts and reproductive state. Extra mucus can be churned out to repulse predators. This wonder gel is solid at rest and liquid under pressure, and can absorb one hundred times its own volume of water—if you try to wash it off, you'll multiply your problem. Wipe off as much as you can with a dry cloth instead. Snail slime is even used in creams and lotions with claims of healing skin and improving its texture.

Garden slugs and snails are hermaphrodites, capable of fertilizing their own eggs, but they generally exchange sperm with a partner. Batches of small, translucent eggs are laid underneath soil.

GARDEN SNAIL
(shell to 1 ½ inches wide)

This common snail, a scourge of California gardens, was brought over intentionally from France in the 1850s for food. It's not the traditional escargot snail but is quite adaptable and farmed as a delicacy in many countries—where it has likewise escaped and spread.

A tough, brown-banded shell protects the snail from predators and the elements. When the weather is too hot or too cold, it can seal the shell with a drum-tight layer of mucus; if it's *really* cold it can add another layer inside the first, like a double-paned window, and can remain dormant for several months. As a snail grows, it adds on to the edge of its shell, so it's always a perfect fit.

A Garden Snail's courtship and mating can last for several hours. After circling, touching tentacles, and nipping at one another, each snail stabs a "love dart" into its partner before transferring sperm. This short, sharp spine is coated with a chemical-laced mucus that allows more of the sperm to survive—an important adaptation in a species that mates with many individuals and stores sperm for later use (or digests it). It's possible that the mythological Cupid and his love arrows were inspired by snails!

GRAY GARDEN SLUG
(to 2 ½ inches long)

The many species of garden slug include the yellow Banana Slug, which can be up to ten inches long. Most are smaller and not as brightly colored, but all share similar lifestyles. A slug has no external shell, so must stay vigilant in its efforts to avoid desiccation, remaining in small crevices (even earthworm holes) during the heat of the day. Right behind its head is a saddle-like mantle with a round pore that opens into the single lung, usually on the slug's right side.

The "Gray" Garden Slug is often spotted, and may be cream-colored, beige, dark brown, or almost black. It's also called Milky Slug, for the whitish slime it produces when agitated. A European hitchhiker from the 1700s, it is now a worldwide agricultural pest, much like the Garden Snail.

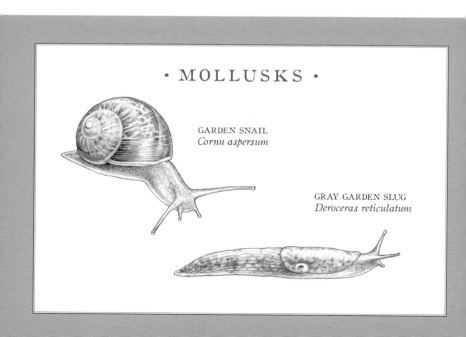

· MOLLUSKS ·

GARDEN SNAIL
Cornu aspersum

GRAY GARDEN SLUG
Deroceras reticulatum

ARTHROPODS

Arthropods (crabs, shrimps, centipedes, insects, spiders, and their ilk) account for well over 80 percent of animal species living today. Their hallmark is a jointed exoskeleton—this tough armor protects them from the elements and some predators. It has also allowed them to evolve all manner of specialized parts: mouthparts that chew, suck, or pierce and that are serrated, curly-straw-like, syringe-style, or sponge-like; powerful legs for crawling, running, climbing, digging, jumping, swimming, and even tasting and hearing; sensitive antennae (short and sweet or long and feathery, they may be used for hearing, tasting, and smelling); and even wings (most insects have them, even if they don't use them). The exoskeleton may be almost any color of the rainbow—helping them to blend in or show off—and smooth and metallic, or thick and coarse.

The exoskeleton has allowed arthropods to become an enormous and extraordinarily diverse group, but it has a major drawback: rigid security means no flexibility for growth. Until it reaches maturity, an arthropod must shed its exoskeleton, or molt, periodically. Inflating itself until the old exoskeleton splits at the seams, it then climbs out and is soft and vulnerable while it waits for the new, bigger exoskeleton to harden.

CENTIPEDE
(1–6 inches long)

Long and flattened, with one pair of legs per segment, a speedy centipede usually shimmies away before you have a chance to count its legs, but it never has the "hundred legs" implied by its name—whether 15 or 177, there's always an odd number of pairs.

A centipede's long antennae help locate prey—it eats anything it can catch (often spiders or insects, but the twelve-inch Amazonian Centipede from South America may choose small mammals, reptiles, or birds). The first pair of legs is modified into venomous "jaws" that seize and paralyze; the last pair of legs can help subdue or carry the quarry. Some centipedes are capable of delivering a painful bite, but they are generally harmless to people. Even the rather frightening-looking House Centipede is beneficial for indoor pest control.

Mostly nocturnal, centipedes are easily dehydrated, so must keep to moist spaces under bark, leaf litter, stones, or logs.

MILLIPEDE
(½ inch to 6 inches long)

Long, leggy, and living in the same damp habitats, millipedes and centipedes are often confused, but have distinct differences. For one, millipedes are not flattened—many are downright cylindrical. With two pairs of legs per segment, a millipede often has more legs than a centipede, but this

· ARTHROPODS I ·

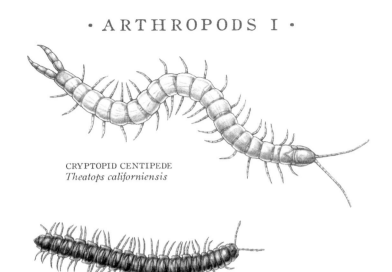

CRYPTOPID CENTIPEDE
Theatops californiensis

GREENHOUSE MILLIPEDE
Oxidus gracilis

PILLBUG
Armadillidium vulgare

SOWBUG
Porcellio scaber

slowpoke glides along smoothly, its myriad short legs moving in wavelike formations. If disturbed, it coils up and can't hurt a fly: a scavenger that dines on decaying plants, a millipede is an essential contributor to soil health. Its only defense is a noxious odor (often cyanide-based) to deter predators like moles, frogs, lizards, and beetles, and possibly to prevent infection by bacteria and fungi.

Greenhouse Millipedes are native to Japan, but are common most everywhere in leaf litter, soil, basements (where they often dry out and die), and greenhouses, where they will eat young plants if they run out of dead material. A "flat-backed" millipede, its profile is still more rounded than a centipede's. A newly-hatched Greenhouse Millipede has only three pairs of legs—it adds legs and segments each time it molts, until it boasts a total of sixty-four legs if it's female or sixty-two if it's male.

PILLBUGS AND SOWBUGS
(to ¾ inch)

Pillbugs, sowbugs, potato bugs, roly-polies, wood lice—what do you call these little guys? Originally from Europe, some delightful British nicknames are bibble-bugs, tiggy-hogs, cheeselogs, chuggypigs, and billy buttons! Most people find them more likable than the average "bug"—maybe because they aren't insects. Related to crabs and lobsters, they are one of a handful of crustaceans who have successfully colonized land. Their ties to water are still strong: tough shell plates discourage small predators but don't protect them from drying out; gill-like breathing structures must be kept moist to avoid suffocation. Pillbugs and sowbugs avoid bright light, moving toward dark spaces that are likely cooler, wetter, and protected from predators.

Creeping pillbugs roll up into little armored balls when disturbed; a flattened shape and two taillike projections prevent sowbugs from rolling up—but they can run! Both are decomposers, primarily eating decaying plant material; they also recycle hard-to-find nutrients by eating their molts for calcium, and their own feces for copper compounds (that tint their blood blue) and bacteria to aid digestion.

Pillbugs and sowbugs molt half their exoskeleton at a time, so one end is pinkish and the other half gray or brown until the process is complete. The occasional orange specimen may be found, as well as pillbugs and sowbugs with a viral infection that inhibits their dark-seeking habits and shortens their lives, but turns them a lovely purple hue.

A female pillbug or sowbug keeps her fertilized eggs swimmingly safe in a fluid-filled pouch called a marsupium. After several weeks, tiny, white young hatch, but remain in the pouch for a few more days before crawling out on their own.

INSECTS

From a microscopic fairyfly to a thirteen-inch stick insect, from a crawling caterpillar to a flea that jumps fifty times its own length, from bees who live their entire lives in the hive to butterflies that migrate thousands of miles: roughly three-quarters of the creatures on earth are insects—and that's just the ones we know about. Insects possess jointed exoskeletons like other arthropods, but with an upgrade: a waxy waterproof outer layer that retains water and allows them to expand beyond the wet environs of many of their relatives. Insects inhabit every place on the planet except the oceans, which are populated by their close kin, the crustaceans (crabs, lobsters, shrimps, and the like).

Insects grow to adulthood in a process called metamorphosis. Grasshoppers, crickets, cockroaches, and a few others undergo incomplete metamorphosis: young nymphs look like wingless miniature adults. With each molt, the wing buds grow a little larger until they are full size at maturity.

The vast majority of insects undergo complete metamorphosis, in which a tiny, ravenous, wormlike larva hatches from an egg. It eats a prodigious amount, often many times its own weight every day—and grows just as quickly, molting several times. At full size, it molts one last time, becoming a pupa. This only appears to be a quiet, restful stage—the process going on inside is anything but: many of the larva's tissues are digested into a nutrient soup! It's more complicated than that, of course—some of the larva's organs stay intact, growing and changing. Even more fascinating—tiny structures called imaginal discs kick into gear. They were present inside the larva as hollow sacs, like microscopic empty balloons, one for each of the adult legs, wings, eyes, antennae, et cetera. During pupation, the discs turn inside out and elongate, using the building blocks from the "soup" to grow and differentiate into the appropriate body parts.

This miracle of transformation is another of the keys to insects' great success: the stages don't compete with each other for food or habitat. Larvae (stomachs with legs) eat and grow quickly and in relative safety, allowing adults to focus on mating and dispersal. And those adults have the senses and locomotion to do it. Besides wings and three pairs of legs for first-class transportation, the three segments of the adult insect (head, thorax, and abdomen) are loaded with equipment that make our five senses seem rather primitive.

Two large compound eyes generate a pixilated view of the world in almost 360 degrees. Many insects can see polarized light and wavelengths that we cannot (such as ultraviolet). Simple eyes—often three, located on the forehead—detect changes in light.

Insect antennae are sensitive to gravity and wind for balance and orientation during flight. They are endowed with a sense of touch and also detect temperature, humidity, sounds as subtle as the beating wings of a potential mate, smells of food or phero-mones (often from great distances)—and some antennae can even taste.

While many insects taste with their mouthparts or antennae, a great number of them can also perceive flavors with their feet! It seems odd, but insects often land on potential food, so taste-sensitive feet can quickly determine what's good to eat.

In addition to their remarkable exoskeletons, phenomenal sensory equipment, and versatile life cycles, insects are gener-ally small—making it easy to flit away, hide in small spaces, and survive on small quantities of food. They are able to commu-nicate via sounds and scents (pheromones). And their ability to reproduce is astounding. One estimation shows a pair of common House Flies giving rise to over 191 quintillion (that's 191 with 18 zeros) flies in five months, if all the offspring lived. Good thing so many creatures like to feast on insects.

The measurements given below refer to the length of the insect's body.

PRAYING MANTIS
(to 5 inches)

With its triangular head, elongate "neck" and body, and front legs folded like a devotee in prayer, a praying mantis is rarely confused with any other insect. Bright green to tan, it's well camouflaged with its plant perch, so you may not see it, but it sees you! Many species are ambush predators: motionless except for a rotating head, they rely on high-resolution, 3-D vision to stalk their insect prey, then strike with lightning-fast reflexes, the spikes on the front legs holding the hapless victim securely while the mantis eats it alive.

Formidable predators, female praying mantises have a reputation for eating a male (or just his head) before, during, or after mating. That's certainly common in captivity, but a well-fed female is unlikely to eat her smaller partner. She'll usually allow him to do a mating dance, climb onto her, deposit his sperm packet, and leave safely. If she does decide to eat him, the nutrients in his body go to a good cause: providing for his offspring. The eggs are laid in a foamy packet that dries and overwinters, until between twelve and four hundred miniature mantises emerge, ready to hunt, in mid-spring.

COMMON EARWIG
(to ⅝ inch)

It's likely that earwigs were originally called ear*wings* for human-ear-shaped wings, folded like fans to fit underneath short, leathery forewings. But they rarely fly, and are better known from folktales claiming they crawl into people's ears and pierce eardrums, or cause insanity (or death) by tunneling into their brains. The pincerlike cerci are definitely fearsome, especially when an earwig bends them over its head, scorpion-style, toward you. This display, along with a foul-smelling secretion, deters most would-be predators. In fact, the cerci are harmless, used for mating rituals, grooming, catching prey, and refolding wings after flight. Males have large, curved, and toothed cerci; the females' are straight and stout.

Earwigs prefer close quarters, under bark or potted plants, between flower petals or sheets of newspaper. They chew on flowers and leaves, but do more good than harm by eating aphids and other teeny insect pests.

A female earwig proves to be a surprisingly devoted mother, at least at first. She digs a shallow nest and busily tends to her cluster of eggs, keeping them safe and clean throughout the winter. Come spring, she hovers protectively over the nymphs, bringing food home until their first molt—when they begin to wander at night and return to safety in the morning. After the second molt, however, they're on their own, as their loving mom is likely to gobble up any who hang around!

CONVERGENT LADY BEETLE
(to ⅓ inch)

Not all ladybugs are ladies, and they aren't even bugs (unlike the aphid and scale insect pests they devour). Ladybugs are actually beetles—entomologists call them ladybird beetles or lady beetles. Revered by farmers at least since the Middle Ages, they were known as the Beetles of Our Lady.

The Convergent Lady Beetle is the most common species in North America, but there are hundreds of others—the shell-like wing covers (which are modified wings) may be yellow to red to black, with any variety of spot patterns, including no spots! The shield behind the head (the pronotum) often carries

29

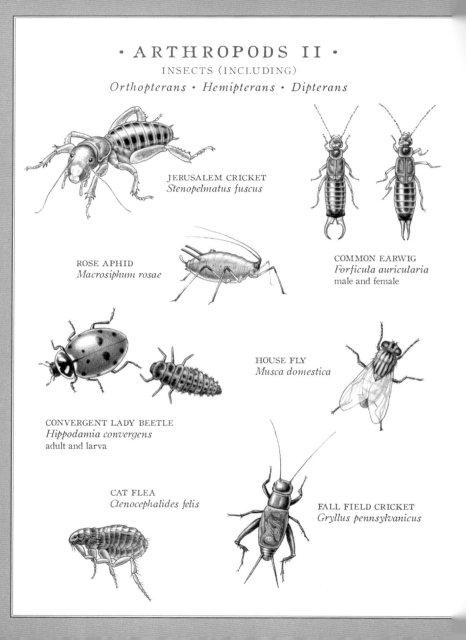

· ARTHROPODS II ·

INSECTS (INCLUDING)

Orthopterans · Hemipterans · Dipterans

JERUSALEM CRICKET
Stenopelmatus fuscus

COMMON EARWIG
Forficula auricularia
male and female

ROSE APHID
Macrosiphum rosae

HOUSE FLY
Musca domestica

CONVERGENT LADY BEETLE
Hippodamia convergens
adult and larva

CAT FLEA
Ctenocephalides felis

FALL FIELD CRICKET
Gryllus pennsylvanicus

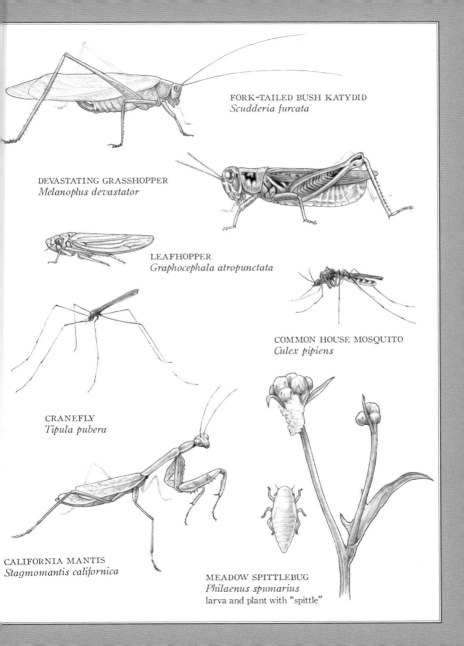

FORK-TAILED BUSH KATYDID
Scudderia furcata

DEVASTATING GRASSHOPPER
Melanoplus devastator

LEAFHOPPER
Graphocephala atropunctata

COMMON HOUSE MOSQUITO
Culex pipiens

CRANEFLY
Tipula pubera

CALIFORNIA MANTIS
Stagmomantis californica

MEADOW SPITTLEBUG
Philaenus spumarius
larva and plant with "spittle"

distinctive markings: Convergent Lady Beetles wear up to thirteen spots—some are completely spotless—but all display two converging white lines on the pronotum.

Lady beetle larvae look like tiny black alligators and have voracious appetites to match—they consume unhatched eggs or each other if there aren't enough aphids. Adults will eat nectar or pollen, and even plant parts, if prey is scarce. When little food is available, or if temperatures are too low or high, they stop reproducing and huddle together under tree branches, leaf litter, or rocks, or in your wall. Convergent Lady Beetles overwinter in particularly large numbers, emerging in busy bright-red swarms when the sun warms their hiding place.

Besides enlisting warning coloration and a noxious taste and odor, lady beetles, when attacked, play dead and "reflex bleed," leaking a bit of bitter, stinky blood from their leg joints. Still, some bird and insect predators will dine on them if given a chance.

CAT FLEA
(to 1/16 inch)

This common flea feeds on the blood of domestic mammals, including cats, dogs, opossums, and rats. Fleas bite people, often causing itchy bumps, but can't complete their life cycle on humans. Highly specialized for a parasitic lifestyle, a flea is wingless, with mouthparts that pierce and suck, and grasping claws on the tips of its legs. A narrow, flattened form and hard body plates with backward-pointing spines make it challenging to catch as it scurries between dense hairs, and tough to squash even if captured.

How does such a minuscule beast overtake a moving host? Powerful hind legs propel it an impressive fifty times its body length, and over a foot high. Up until recently, fleas were thought to be the best jumpers for their size, but experiments have shown that spittlebugs are the true champions.

White, oval, almost microscopic flea eggs laid on a cat's fur drop onto the rug or grass (wherever the cat sleeps). Wormlike larvae, less than an eighth of an inch long, eat just about anything organic, including feces from adult fleas, with chewing mouthparts. They spin sticky silken cocoons, and after about four days are ready to emerge—but if conditions aren't perfect, they can wait for many months. Warmth or humidity, vibration (like footsteps, hopefully not yours), and an increase in carbon dioxide trigger emergence: within seconds, a young flea hops onto its first host and prepares to feast.

Orthopterans

The orthopterans are named for their "straight wings" (just as an orthodontist straightens teeth), which lie folded at rest. Most grasshoppers, crickets, and katydids also have long hind legs for jumping, and are herbivorous, with chewing mouthparts. There's hardly a bird, mammal, amphibian, or reptile who doesn't enjoy orthopterans as a tasty treat.

Grasshopper, crickets, and katydids all "stridulate," meaning they produce sounds by rubbing legs and/or wings together— with each species having its own distinctive tune. You will only hear them calling during a particular season, since most groups have but one generation a year. Usually it's just the males who croon, but some species have singing females as well.

GRASSHOPPER
(to 2 ¾ inches)

A grasshopper's excellent camouflage keeps it well hidden—until it's disturbed and startles you with an explosive jump and a flash (and sometimes clicking) of wings. The long legs work like catapults and are also used for music: spurs on a grasshopper's hind legs rub over a scraper on its wings, sounding much like a fingernail running over the teeth of a comb. A female hears the male's fiddling serenade with the tympanum on her abdomen, and once she's mated, she uses her multipurpose ovipositor to probe the ground for the perfect spot to dig a little burrow and lay her eggs.

Many grasshoppers are strong fliers, using large, membranous hind wings to escape from predators, or for migration. The legendary swarms of crop-devastating locusts are a phase that some species of grasshopper exhibit in response to overcrowding, but conditions have to be just right.

Grasshoppers can spit out a bit of noxious brown fluid (called tobacco juice by some) when they are mishandled. Harmless to humans, it's just icky enough to put off smaller hunters.

KATYDID
(to 2 ½ inches)

At first glance, katydids look like grasshoppers with long filamentous antennae. Their wings are leaflike—complete with veins—and come in subtle shades of green or brown. The wingless nymphs of some species have extra-long, black-and-white-striped legs and antennae, like exotic tropical shrimps. Most katydids eat leaves; some nymphs may also chew into fruits.

A male katydid sings with his wings, rubbing a scraper on

one against a file on the other to make ticking, zipping, buzzing, or chirping sounds, depending on the species—in some, the females (recognized by their flattened, hook-shaped ovipositors) respond in kind to the males' calls. Katydids hear with a tympanum on each front leg.

FIELD CRICKET
(to 1 inch)

A quintessential summer night includes the peaceful chirping of male field crickets as they stroke a scraper on one wing along a row of teeth on the other. A female hears the lovely songs with a tympanum on each of her front legs, and locates the musician of her choice.

A cricket may be tan to black, with a round head, long thin antennae, jumping legs, and stout, spinelike sensory cerci on its abdomen. Between her cerci, a female has a long ovipositor, which she inserts deep into the soil or a plant stem to keep her eggs safe through the winter. Adults hide in crevices near buildings or under rocks or leaves. In cooler months, they may find their way into your warm house, where they can damage furniture or clothing—as omnivores, they eat most anything, including each other if they are really hungry.

Kept as lucky charms in China, Japan, and parts of Europe, crickets are also bred as food for both people and pets around the world.

JERUSALEM CRICKET
(to 2 inches)

Looking like a colossal, pale ant with a striped abdomen, the Jerusalem Cricket has many common names that refer to its large head—Old Bald-Headed Man, Skull Insect, and Child's Face are notable examples. This strange beast is not from Jerusalem, and is not a true cricket—it's wingless, with sturdy, spiny legs adapted for digging instead of jumping. Docile and slow-moving, it spends most of its life underground, coming out at night in search of food, and in the spring, for mates.

It can bite you with its formidable mouthparts, but a Jerusalem Cricket would rather run away and keep chewing on roots and tubers (another common name is potato bug), as well as any other vegetable, fruit, or meat (including beetle larvae, earthworms, and other Jerusalem Crickets).

A Jerusalem Cricket doesn't sing like its relatives: it communicates by beating the ground with its abdomen like a drum. It's not unusual for the female to eat the male after mating; afterwards, she digs a chamber at the end of a burrow, then lines it with a papery, birdlike "nest" for her eggs.

Hemipterans

Watch out who you call a bug—all bugs are insects, but not all insects are bugs. Hemipterans are the "true bugs," a group that includes water boatmen, Bedbugs, cicadas, scale insects, whiteflies, aphids, and leafhoppers. There are swimmers, water skaters, fliers, jumpers, and walkers in this group, but all have piercing and sucking mouthparts. Bedbugs are parasites that suck blood, and there are a few predatory hemipterans, but most of these insects feed on plant sap.

Some sap suckers excrete excess water, sugars, and amino acids as sweet honeydew. This often drips onto leaves, the ground, or your car, making them sticky and sometimes encouraging sooty mold growth. Honeydew may be collected by ants, bees, or wasps as a food source; in fact, some ants will actively "milk" aphids, mealybugs, or scale insects, gathering and eating the honeydew as well as protecting their "livestock" from predators and parasites—even carrying the bugs from wilted plants to fresh ones.

LEAFHOPPER
(to ⅝ inch)

You may notice what looks like a colorful grain of rice on your sleeve or a leaf—when you reach for it, it quickly runs sideways, or blasts off, gone in a twinkling. The pale, translucent nymphs and brightly colored or camouflaged adults both feed on the sap of weeds, grass, and garden or crop plants, preferring moist, new growth. They don't usually occur in high enough numbers to do much damage, although they can spread disease from one plant to another. Predators (like lady beetles and spiders) and parasites (like wasps) abound.

APHID
(to 3/16 inch)

A tiny, plump, wingless aphid may be pink, green, black, or brown. Usually stock-still with mouthparts sucking away, it moves slowly and rarely leaves the plant on which it was born. Its soft body is unarmed against the elements, infection (by bacteria, viruses, or fungi), and insect predators—lady beetles find it particularly toothsome.

In some species, two thin cornicles (tubes) protruding from the abdomen produce a waxy substance unpalatable to predators, and aphids are often protected by ants while harvesting honeydew. However, aphids' main line of defense is their extraordinarily rapid and unusual mode of reproduction. Many species are parthenogenic for part of their life cycle: a female produces clones of herself, without mating, and often these young are born live (instead of laid as eggs). Each matures quickly and gives birth to her own generations of clones—one aphid can give rise to billions of descendants. When a plant becomes overcrowded, or food becomes limited, a female gives birth to winged females who disperse to other plants to start the cycle anew. In autumn, the strategy changes—the female produces males *and* females, who find mates (mixing up the gene pool, finally!) and lay eggs that will hatch the following spring.

SPITTLEBUG
(to ⅜ inch)

The white, foamy, spit-like mass on your rosemary or strawberry plants isn't actually saliva, but you may not find comfort in the knowledge there is a tiny bug (or three) in the middle of it: a spittlebug nymph. Instead of generating honeydew, the nymph uses excess fluid from the plant sap it slurps to create frothy bubbles that hide and protect its delicate body from heat, cold, sun, and would-be diners.

Upon maturity, the rather inconspicuous gray or brownish adult insect leaves the safety of the spittle and catapults itself to new plants: huge muscles in a spittlebug's hind legs store energy that, when released, shoot it up to one hundred times its body length and well over two feet in the air, leaving the flea's jumping record in the dust. For its size, the spittlebug is the highest-jumping animal. Humans jump with a force about three times that of gravity, or 3 Gs; a spittlebug is subjected to the force of over 400 Gs. Good luck catching one of these!

Dipterans

The thousands of species of flies all consume liquid diets, from nectar to blood. Unlike most insects, flies have only one pair of wings; the second pair of wings has evolved into halteres, each a tiny stem with a knob at the end. Beating counter to the wings' rhythm, they act as a sophisticated gyroscopic balancing system to stabilize flight.

CRANE FLY
(to 1 inch)

When it's not mistaken for a giant mosquito, the crane fly is often called a mosquito hawk, mosquito-eater, or skeeter-eater. These gentle behemoths can't hurt a mosquito, much less a person—their mouthparts are too delicate to bite; in fact, many do not eat at all, only living a few days. They have a clumsy bouncing flight, and long dangly legs that detach easily (good for escaping from birds, bats, cats, and spiderwebs). If one is perched on the wall, step in close to see its large, knobbed halteres, right behind the wings.

The many *Tipula* species have different body and wing patterns, and come in a whole range of sizes. Most lay eggs in damp soil. The wriggly larvae, whose tough, brown skins earn them the hooliganish name leatherjackets, feed on decaying vegetation—though a couple of introduced species are lawn pests who nibble on grass and its roots.

HOUSE MOSQUITO
(to ⅜ inch)

Is there anything worse than that high-pitched buzzing in your ear when you're trying to sleep? Well, maybe the itchy red bumps that come later! Most house mosquitoes actually prefer to bite birds or other mammals, but in a city, there are lots of people, and we attract them with lights at dusk, carbon dioxide in our breath, chemicals in our sweat, and our body heat. They can't resist! Luckily, all life stages of the mosquito are equally delectable to a whole variety of fishes, birds, amphibians, bats, and small mammals, so we have allies in keeping the biters at bay.

Adult mosquitoes eat nectar, honeydew, and fruit juice; but after a female mates, she needs protein to produce eggs, and she develops a craving for blood (instead of ice cream and pickles). Once she finds a suitable victim, she unsheathes six needlelike mouthparts from her long, flexible proboscis to cut into and grip the flesh while she probes for a blood vessel, injects a bit of saliva, and sucks up blood. The trouble comes from the multipurpose saliva—while it expands the blood vessels, keeps blood from clotting, and numbs the site, it also causes an allergic reaction (swelling and itching) for many people.

Once she's filled with blood, the female mosquito lays her eggs on the surface of standing water—rain gutters, buckets, pet bowls—anywhere that water puddles. The squirmy "wiggler" larvae develop into tumbling pupae. The cycle from egg to adult can be as short as a week. A male doesn't have a long proboscis and can't bite, and he's easily distinguished by his noticeably bushy female-finding antennae. He considers the whine of her flight quite alluring.

HOUSE FLY
(to ½ inch)

Originally from Central Asia, the House Fly is found everywhere humans live. Larger, colorful green bottle and blue bottle flies also show up on household trash or decaying meat;

the common House Fly is more understated, with a pale, yellowish abdomen, a gray or black thorax sporting four stripes, and deep red eyes. Look for space between the eyes to identify a female; the eyes of a male almost touch.

Powerful fliers with a keen sense of sight, House Flies can perceive faster movements than we can, so they are particularly hard to swat; minute claws and sticky footpads permit them to walk on almost any surface, and even upside down.

House Flies have an affection for garbage, rotting food, and feces, with the table manners to match. After smelling a potential meal during flight (using its antennae), a fly lands on the food to taste it with hairs on its feet. A fly can't bite or chew—its sponge-like mouthparts can only slurp up fluids, so if it's solid fare, the fly liquefies it with saliva. The fly takes in so much food that it is constantly defecating—and it doesn't mind pooping on our meals.

House Flies lay eggs in the same things they eat. White, legless maggots burrow in, and before pupating, crawl someplace warm and dry. To escape its pupa, a young fly inflates a pouch, like a little airbag, from its forehead and pops off the end of the pupal case. The pouch deflates back into its head, and after about two days, the fly is ready to mate—a female need only mate once to fertilize the five hundred or so eggs she will lay over the following few days.

Despite their unsavory reputation, House Flies play an important role as scavengers, recycling nutrients from manure and from dead and decaying plants and animals.

41

Lepidopterans

Elegant, graceful butterflies are the most beloved insects; less admired are their more lackluster kin, the moths—though moths aren't all as plain as you might think, and they outnumber the butterflies in species by ten to one. Both belong to the order Lepidoptera, meaning "scale-wings," so named for thousands of tiny overlapping scales on the surface of their wings, providing insulation, waterproofing, and a dazzling array of colors and patterns for camouflage or warning, to startle predators or attract mates. Rubbing some of the powdery scales off may make the insect less aerodynamic but does not kill it. Butterflies and moths naturally shed some scales when brushing against flowers, mating, and flying—and the scales help them slip out of the grasp of a predator.

There are some general differences between the two groups, but these do not apply to every species. A typical butterfly is solar-powered, so is active during sunny days. It holds its showy wings vertically when at rest, but will spread them out to warm in the sun: the more intense colors on the wings' upper sides absorb heat better. It cannot hear, uses sight to find mates and flowers, has knobs at the tips of its antennae, and pupates as a dangling chrysalis. A moth is usually nocturnal, so it must generate heat when it flies; its larger scales make it stout and fluffy, possibly to conserve that warmth. Threadlike or feathery antennae allow it to locate mates and food by smell and vibrations (hearing) in the dark. Wings (often drab-colored) are held horizontally or folded against its body at rest, and the pupa lies tucked in the ground (or a plant's stem) or nestled in a silken cocoon.

While we are enamored of fluttering lepidopteran adults, their juicy, protein-rich larvae (caterpillars) are more tantalizing to other animals. Particularly attractive to parasitoid wasps and flies, they are also a large part of most baby birds' diets, and are terribly tempting to any number of mammals, reptiles, amphibians, and other insects. Food for people in some parts of the world, caterpillars turn the tables and like to eat *our* food with their sturdy jaws—they can be highly destructive to food crops.

Look carefully at a caterpillar and you will see two types of legs: three pairs of thin, hook-like true legs up front, and behind those, two to five pairs of stumpy prolegs for walking and holding on with patches of Velcro-like bristles at the tips. Also look for tiny breathing holes along the sides of its body, one on each segment.

Behind impressive chewing mouthparts, a caterpillar has a silk-producing spinneret. Many butterfly larvae form a little silk button from which they hang their chrysalis. Some caterpillars use silk strands to hide themselves in a leaf or as a safety line when dropping to the ground to avoid a predator, and many moth pupae spin a protective cocoon. The most famous of these are silkworms, whose unwound cocoons are woven into fabric.

Voracious, lumbering caterpillars give rise to wispy butterflies and moths, whose eating habits, though not always their food sources, are equally dainty. Almost all have a long, tubelike proboscis for sipping liquids—oftentimes nectar from flowers, making them important pollinators. Butterflies prefer colorful flowers that aren't blue or green; moth species that are strictly nocturnal pollinate fragrant white night-blooming flowers. Not all their sustenance comes from posies, however: moths and butterflies may drink honeydew or tree sap and visit wet sand, mud, rotting fruit, dung, carrion, sweaty socks, or puddles of water, looking for minerals and moisture.

· ARTHROPODS III ·

INSECTS

Lepidopterans

BILOBED SEMILOOPER
Megalographa biloba
(*see* INCHWORM)

BUCKEYE
Junonia coenia

CABBAGE WHITE
Pieris rapae

GULF FRITILLARY
Agraulis vanillae

FIERY SKIPPER
Hylephila phyleus

WEST COAST LADY
Vanessa annabella

SALT MARSH TIGER
Estigmene acraea
(*see* WOOLLY BEAR)

MONARCH
Danaus plexippus

WESTERN TIGER SWALLOWTAIL
Papilio rutulus

GRAY HAIRSTREAK
Strymon melinus

Included here are a couple of moth larvae you will see in the daytime, and a tiny taste of the many common backyard butterflies. There is tremendous variation in size, pattern, and coloration, even of the same species, depending on gender, season, and even availability of water. If you become particularly enamored of these winged enchanters, a dedicated butterfly and moth field guide may be in order. Caterpillars are shown if you are likely to spy them.

The sizes below refer to the moth or butterfly's wingspan or the length of the caterpillar.

CABBAGE WHITE
(to 2 inches)

Introduced to the United States from Europe around the turn of the century, the Cabbage White is the most common butterfly in the world. Starting in the early spring, you'll see these white beauties fluttering around just about everywhere. Keep an eye out for their lilting, spiraling courtship dance. The female has two black spots on each forewing; the male has one. As the name implies, a Cabbage White lays her eggs on plants in the cabbage family, where the larvae bore in and get to their job of eating. Full grown at about an inch long, the green larvae may be found in your cabbage, kale, or broccoli. As with many butterflies, there are several generations in a year; at the end of the season, the chrysalis overwinters.

WESTERN TIGER SWALLOWTAIL
(to 4 inches)

This large, attractive butterfly's forked appearance is due to the "tails" on the hind wings, reminiscent of a swallow's tail. Looking at its adult form, elegantly striped in yellow and black, with blue and orange spots, you'd never guess it once looked like a bird dropping! As the caterpillar grows, it changes from merely unappetizing to rather scary-looking: eyespots glare out from a green body, creating the illusion of a big head.

This frightens predators and distracts them from the tiny real head at the tip of the caterpillar. And it has another trick up its  neck—if disturbed, the caterpillar will suddenly hunch up its false head and protrude two bright orange, smelly stinkhorns, scaring off anything that wasn't put off by being stared down. Even the ants, spiders, and praying mantises who might not mind the snake impression are repulsed by the strong smell.

The related, but slightly smaller, Anise Swallowtail has a striped and spotted caterpillar (also with stinkhorns), and prefers plants in the fennel family to the trees that the Western Tiger Swallowtail is so fond of.

BUCKEYE
(to 2 ¾ inches)

The Buckeye employs eyespots like the Swallowtail's, but they're worn by the adults. Under wraps when the butterfly is resting with its wings held vertically, the flash and sudden appearance of a bunch of eyes is sure to startle a lurking predator. The Buckeye's caterpillar doesn't need scare tactics—it feasts on plants containing bitter compounds (including plantains and snapdragons), and incorporates them into its body, rendering itself virtually inedible. One look at the bristly black-and-white larva and its bright-orange head is warning enough!

The territorial male Buckeye can be quite feisty, challenging not just other butterflies, but any large insect, and even passing birds.

Like several species covered here, this butterfly looks like it has only two pairs of legs—the front pair is short and tucked up against the body.

WEST COAST LADY
(to 2 ¼ inches)

This pretty little orange-and-brown butterfly has bright blue-and-white spots. Its larvae are particularly fond of host plants in the mallow family (including hollyhocks and cheeseweed) and also eat stinging nettles! In fact, the caterpillars look a bit like nettles themselves—light brown to black with yellow patterning, they are completely covered with spiny, branching prickles.

If you've ever raised caterpillars in a butterfly kit, chances are they were Painted Lady butterflies, a close relative of the West Coast Lady; the Red Admiral is another common relation.

MONARCH
(to 4 inches)

The most familiar North American butterfly, the large, handsome Monarch was so named by early settlers after King William III, whose royal colors were orange and black. The bold coloration is a warning to birds: "I don't taste good!" Monarch caterpillars feed only on milkweed plants; the bitter compounds assimilated into their bodies make birds of many species sick (plenty of other birds, rodents, and insects still seem to find them appetizing).

The splendid Monarch caterpillar, with black, yellow, and white stripes and a pair of black sensory "tentacles" at each end, becomes an elegant jade chrysalis with a thin black stripe and spots of glittering gold.

A male Monarch is slightly larger than a female, with narrower, more brownish wing veins and a black spot on each hind wing. Related butterflies use pheromones from this spot to attract mates, but Monarchs don't seem to need them; instead the male chases a female and grasps her in midair, and they fall to the ground to mate.

The swooping flight of a Monarch does more than transport it from one flower to the next. Unable to withstand freezing winter temperatures, Monarchs migrate by the millions every year. Some populations remain within California or Florida; others travel thousands of miles from Canada to Mexico. In cooler places, they cluster together to keep warm, enveloping trees with living foliage. Come spring, these butterflies head north, but won't survive to make it to their northernmost range. This may take three or four more generations—the spring and early summer groups only live about five weeks (the larger, heartier overwintering batch lives eight months or more). How they perform this incredible trip without a GPS is not completely understood, although the position of the sun and the magnetic pull of the earth play important roles.

GULF FRITILLARY
(to 3 ¾ inches)

This tropical species only breeds on particular types of passionflower vines growing in California, the southern United States, and farther south, through Central and South America. They fly to the warmest parts of their range to overwinter. Where common, you can find all stages of the life cycle on the same plant, from tiny egg to mating adults. The adult's long, narrow wings are bright orange with black markings and

white spots on top; iridescent silvery streaks adorn the undersides. The shiny orange caterpillar (sometimes with lavender stripes) is covered in rows of dangerous-looking branched black spines, but their bark is worse than their bite: they are soft and flexible.

GRAY HAIRSTREAK
(to 1 ¼ inches)

A quick, zippy flight habit makes it difficult for predators to track this common butterfly; when resting, it often rubs its silvery hind wings together, drawing attention to bright orange eyespots and antenna-like "hairs," possibly fooling would-be diners to attack the wrong end of the butterfly. The tip of the abdomen is orange in males, gray in females. Pale pink to green, depending on what flowers or fruit it is feeding on, the sluglike larva can produce honeydew, attracting ants that protect it from predators and parasitoids.

FIERY SKIPPER
(to 1 ½ inches)

The Fiery Skipper breeds on grass in lawns—how's that for urban? The larvae eat the blades and roll themselves up in the leaves, securing their shelters with silk, so it's unusual to see them. Skippers are named for a rapid, darting flight pattern, and their short antennae (usually tipped with hooked clubs), stocky bodies, large eyes, and small wings distinguish them from typical butterflies. Most come in shades of gray and brown and are difficult to identify, but the bright yellow-orange hue of a male Fiery Skipper sets him apart. Females sport a more subdued yellow-brown tint.

INCHWORM
(to 1 ½ inches long)

Most people find inchworms irresistibly delightful, with their characteristic looping gait. With no legs between the true legs up front and the two or three prolegs at its back end, an inchworm has to hunch its middle to bring the rear legs up to meet its front end before it can extend forward. Inchworms (or measuring worms, loopers, or semiloopers, as they are called depending on region and species) are the larvae of geometer ("earth-measure") moths, a large group of small, inconspicuous moths. Green or brown to blend in with its host plant (which could be your broccoli or kale), an inchworm may respond to a disturbance by impersonating a twig—standing stock-still balanced on its prolegs—or it may suddenly drop off its perch, only to pull itself up by a silken safety line later.

WOOLLY BEAR
(to 2 inches long)

There are a number of tiger moths with bristly caterpillars called woolly bears. Charming little fellows, they curl up into balls when disturbed, and should be handled gently—some people's skin is irritated by the "fur" on these "bears." The Salt Marsh Caterpillar can range from pale yellow to almost black, and you'll often see the last generation in the autumn as they creep around the ground, looking for places to overwinter. In the spring, they pupate and become Salt Marsh Tigers.

Tiger moths are a diverse and colorful group, and the Salt Marsh Tiger is no exception. It is snow white with black spots and black-striped legs and antennae; the top of its abdomen is brilliant orange, and the male's hind wings are yellow orange. The adults don't last long—only living three to five days, they are devoted to one thing: mating. Their efforts are so concentrated that they don't even eat! The evening after he emerges

 from his cocoon, a male inflates two curved, furry pheromone-bearing organs, the coremata, from his abdomen. Fully unspooled, they can be as long as the moth. The heavy

scent attracts both males and females—the new males unfurl their coremata in turn and engage in an energetic (and aromatic) group display called a lek. Females fly into the mix and choose a suitor. A few hours after the lek winds down, any unmated female beckons males with her own perfume; the following night, each female lays an impressive four hundred to one thousand eggs.

Hymenopterans

Bees and wasps and ants, oh my! Many people flinch just imagining painful stings and home invasions. Humans aren't the only ones: so many birds and mammals are wary of getting stung that a number of harmless flies and beetles escape predation by masquerading as bees and wasps, employing their distinctive yellow-and-black warning coloration.

The much-maligned stingers are adapted from egg-laying structures, so only females can sting. Honey Bee workers are one of the few hymenopterans that usually die after stinging—others can sting as many times as they like. Yet bees and wasps are not out to get you. Even the aggressive yellowjacket is unlikely to sting unless you swat at or step on it, or threaten its nest.

Most everyone is familiar with the large colonies and

complicated social structures of Honey Bees and ants, but the majority of the hymenopterans are solitary. They sometimes sleep or nest near each other, but there is no cooperation. Solitary or social, the life cycle usually begins the same way: a female emerges from a burrow or leaf litter in the spring. If she mated in the fall, she's ready to start a family; in some species, mating occurs right after emerging from hibernation. The female finds a suitable place for a nest, prepares it with care, stocks it with food, and lays her eggs.

For many solitary hymenopterans, the mother's job is done, but for social species, this batch of eggs is the beginning of a remarkably efficient and organized colony. The mother (the queen) is usually the only fertile female—her daughters are workers, who operate within a strict division of labor: some build and maintain the nest; others take care of the young, gather food, or defend the colony. While they cannot have young of their own, workers can control the destinies of the larvae by how they feed and care for them, even producing new queens when the need arises. Males (drones) are produced from unfertilized eggs. Mating is their sole function, and most die shortly thereafter.

Hymenopteran nests, filled with adults, developing young, and sometimes food stores, are very appealing to the predators that dare attack them. Any number of birds, mammals, rodents, reptiles, amphibians, and insects try to capture some of the bounty—it's no surprise even the most docile hymenopteran will aggressively attack if its hive is threatened. Most bee and wasp nests are active for only one year, and are especially vulnerable to predation in the fall—the queen has left or died, and the remaining members are sluggish in cooler weather, making them a high-protein fast-food meal for a hungry predator.

For the social species, the workers—the most frequently

encountered members of the colony—are depicted. Queens and drones are usually (but not always) slightly larger, with different body proportions, such as a queen's long egg-laying abdomen or a drone's big eyes (the better to see females with).

— Bees —

If you've eaten any fruits, vegetables, or nuts today, give thanks to bees—their visits to flowers start fruit and seed development for at least one-third of our food crops. Flower pollen is the bees' source of protein and other nutrients, and they are built to collect it: branched hairs all over their bodies attract pollen, stiff combs on Honey Bee and bumble bee legs groom it off, and many bees have specialized hairs or segments on their hind legs that function as pollen baskets to carry their food home.

Bees gather nectar (their energy source) using a tubelike proboscis. For blooms that are still too long or thin to reach into, many bees will "nectar rob" the flower, cutting a slit in its base and sipping from the outside.

Of the 20,000 known species of bees, 95 percent are solitary. They include quite a cast of characters, including sweat bees, mason bees, cuckoo bees, leafcutting bees, carpenter bees, and mining bees. Some are tiny or look like flies, and some are bright green—you might not even recognize them as bees. Solitary bees do not produce honey, and they aren't aggressive, since they have no colony to defend.

The last few decades have seen a troubling decline in diversity and abundance of bees in the United States and Europe, due to habitat destruction and fragmentation, pesticide usage, climate change, parasites, pathogens, lack of genetic diversity,

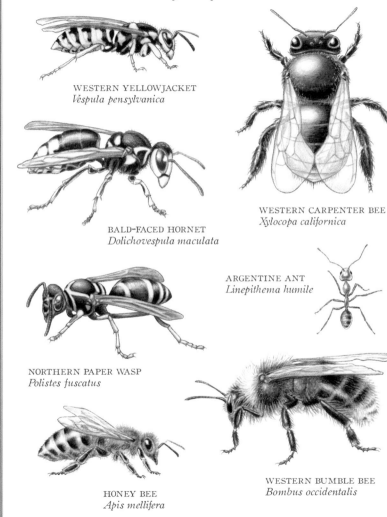

· ARTHROPODS IV ·

INSECTS

Hymenopterans

WESTERN YELLOWJACKET
Vespula pensylvanica

BALD-FACED HORNET
Dolichovespula maculata

WESTERN CARPENTER BEE
Xylocopa californica

ARGENTINE ANT
Linepithema humile

NORTHERN PAPER WASP
Polistes fuscatus

HONEY BEE
Apis mellifera

WESTERN BUMBLE BEE
Bombus occidentalis

and drought. But you can help bees! Home gardens with an array of flowering plants (especially native plants) provide the varied diet that is essential for bees' health, much more nutritious than the monoculture of a big commercial crop.

CARPENTER BEE
(to 1 inch long)

You may notice carpenter bees in your yard because of their large size. They are often mistaken for bumble bees, but their shiny, bare abdomens give them away. Or loud buzzing might grab your attention—their brawny muscles can vibrate pollen right off flowers' anthers! The in-your-face attitude is also hard to ignore—a male circles your head or hovers near your face if you are in his territory (but don't worry, he can't sting). In the spring, a female might approach to see if you're a piece of wood suitable for a nest, but she is not aggressive and won't sting unless you hassle her.

Carpenter bees are named for the tidy round tunnel the female chews into wood with her powerful jaws. Dead branches, fence posts, patio furniture, and decks are not food for the bee, but they provide a safe, dry spot for her eggs. Once she is done excavating, she goes to the end of the tunnel and forms a nutritious pollen and nectar "pillow" on which she lays an egg. Then she uses chewed wood mixed with saliva to construct a particleboard-like wall to seal off the tiny room. She builds six to eight little nursery chambers like this, filling the tube. The provisions are enough to feed the larvae through maturity, so the mother flies off, her work complete.

Eggs destined to become male carpenter bees are laid in the outermost chambers, so males emerge first and remain close, protecting their turf while waiting for females to make their appearance.

The tunneling of western species of carpenter bees is not usually extensive enough to cause structural damage—they reuse existing nests if they can (carving is a lot of work!). If you are bothered by their hole-making, you may provide ready-made tubes for them—⅜-inch holes drilled 6 inches deep into a piece of wood or bundles of thin bamboo stalks make good nests. It's worth it: these native bees are important and efficient pollinators for many types of flowers.

Carpenter bees' large size and food reserves make them attractive prey for ants, termites, reptiles, birds, squirrels, opossums, raccoons, and skunks.

BUMBLE BEE
(to 1 inch long)

Big, fuzzy bumble bees occur almost everywhere in the world, even in the Arctic. Their large size allows them to generate more body heat with their flight muscles, and thick fur helps retain that heat, so they can fly earlier and later in the day during cool weather than most of their bee brethren.

Bumble bees were originally called humble-bees for the humming sound made while flying; "bumble," which also referred to buzzing, probably replaced it because of the lovely alliteration. Some etymologists have traced the origin of the word "bumble" (as in staggering or stumbling) to the bees' clumsy flying style. There's a reason their flight isn't terribly graceful—they are often hefting quite a load! A bumble bee can carry almost its own weight in nectar or about half its weight in pollen.

A bumble bee queen creates a nest lined with moss and dried grass or leaves. Inside, she fashions a small cup, or "honey pot," from wax secreted by glands in her abdomen, and fills it with nectar; she makes a smaller pot for her first eight to ten eggs. Like a tiny hen, she uses her body heat to keep the eggs warm—on cold or rainy days, she stays with them, sipping from the honey pot and eating a reserve of pollen, which she also uses to feed the larvae once they hatch. Such is the modest beginning of a colony that can range from twenty to several hundred bumble bees, depending on the species and food availability. Since the colony will not survive the winter, bumble bees store just a few days' worth of nectar and pollen.

Like carpenter bees, and a number of solitary bees, a bumble bee may employ "buzz pollination," gripping a flower with its legs or mouthparts and using powerful flight muscles to vibrate pollen out. You can hear this when a bumble bee's low buzzing changes to a higher pitch (the frequency is close to the note middle C). While this method is useful for all flowers, it is essential for certain types of plants whose pollen is enclosed in narrow tubelike anthers (tomatoes, peppers, blueberries, and many other wild and cultivated plants).

HONEY BEE
(to ⅝ inch long)

Native to Europe, Asia, and Africa, Honey Bees have been domesticated at least since 2600 BC in Egypt and were introduced to America in the early 1600s by European colonists. Prized for their delicious honey and fragrant beeswax, Honey Bees are, most importantly, pollinators of agricultural crops.

Within a Honey Bee hive, multiple honeycombs of perfectly hexagonal cells house eggs, developing larvae, pupae, and honey. The queen can live from two to seven years. The more times she has mated (usually with ten to twenty drones during her single mating flight), the longer she can lay eggs before the workers raise new queens to replace her. In the spring, the queen bee lays eggs nearly continuously, about two thousand each day! A hive may house as many as sixty thousand bees.

When the hive gets too crowded, the old queen leaves with several thousand workers to start a new colony. This swarm may rest on a tree branch while scout bees look for an ideal location. Swarming usually lasts a day or two, and happens only once or twice a year, when food is plentiful. With full bellies and no hive or brood to defend, swarming bees are rarely aggressive.

Unlike other hymenopterans, Honey Bees maintain a large colony over many seasons, so they require a food supply that lasts through winter, when flowers aren't available: this is why they make honey. Workers regurgitate nectar and special enzymes into cells in the honeycomb and fan their wings, helping to evaporate the water. When the honey is the right concentration, the cells are capped off with wax. It's a precious commodity—one worker produces only about a twelfth of a teaspoon of honey in her four- to six-week life.

In the pitch darkness of the hive, Honey Bees use chemical signals for much communication and recognition. When a worker returns from a successful foraging trip, the flowers' scent lingers on her, giving her hive mates a clue to its origin, but she has a wonderful trick up her sleeve—a "waggle dance." The pattern, duration, and vigorousness of her dancing reveal the nectar's quality and quantity, as well as its distance and direction from the hive.

For proper development, Honey Bee eggs, larvae, and pupae require a constant temperature of 90–95 degrees. Workers collectively fan their wings and gather water to cool the hive on hot days, and cluster together, vibrating their flight muscles to keep things toasty in cold weather.

A Honey Bee worker is the only bee or wasp with a heavily barbed stinger, effective for attacking another insect. But those same barbs usually keep the stinger lodged in a mammal's thick flesh—as the bee flies away, its abdomen ruptures, leaving the stinger, part of the digestive tract, muscles, and a venom sac behind. The bee dies shortly thereafter. Since the muscles continue to pump venom for a minute or so, it's important to remove the stinger as quickly as possible. Scraping it off with a fingernail, credit card, or other flat object works best.

A foraging Honey Bee is unlikely to sting unless stepped on or manhandled; if she's near the hive, she will sacrifice her life to defend the colony. And when she stings, she releases a banana-scented pheromone that attracts and agitates other workers, making them more likely to sting. So if you're stung, beat a hasty retreat!

Many creatures enjoy eating Honey Bees and/or honey. Besides bird, spider, and insect predators, toads have been known to sit at a hive entrance and pick off workers as they enter and exit. Mice and rats will burrow into hives, and larger mammals such as skunks, raccoons, and bears like their honey with some protein (bees) in it.

— Wasps —

Wasps are one of the most despised and least understood groups of insects. Often confused with bees, wasps do not collect pollen or make honey, though they do sip nectar. And when a wasp visits flowers, its smoother, often shiny body doesn't transfer as much pollen as that of a fuzzy bee. Most of the tens of thousands of wasp species found worldwide are solitary. Some build nests in burrows or construct them out of mud; many are parasitoids: they lay their eggs on or inside host insects—which the larvae feed on and eventually kill. Sounds gruesome, but many of these wasps are considered beneficial, as their hosts are agricultural pests; in fact, parasitoid wasps are often released intentionally as natural pest management.

The infamous yellowjackets, hornets, and paper wasps are social members of the wasp family. A social wasp can and will employ its impressive stinger multiple times. Unlike a bee, which only stings defensively, a wasp requires its large stinger for subduing and paralyzing prey, as well as for defense. Social wasps prey heavily on insects and, like the parasitoid wasps, are beneficial in the garden, keeping caterpillars, flies, mosquitoes, and other insect populations in check. If they are not in a highly trafficked area, consider allowing these valuable insects to remain—their nest is usually used for only one year.

While adult social wasps eat only sugary beverages like nectar, juice from rotting fruit, honeydew, and tree sap, their larvae need protein to grow and develop. So the adults capture caterpillars and other insects, which they chew up and feed to the young. The larvae, in turn, exude droplets of a sweet fluid that provides the adults with essential proteins and encourages them to collect more insect meals. As summer draws on, the colony grows larger, and flowers and insect prey become harder to find. This is when paper wasps and yellowjackets will show up at your picnic: your soda (unless it's diet) is a lovely substitute for flower nectar, and larvae are happy with bits of your burger or steak instead of insects. Open garbage cans are attractive for the same reasons—as are the flies that the garbage attracts!

NORTHERN PAPER WASP
(to ¾ inch long)

Many types of wasps build gray paperlike nests from vegetable fibers (rotted or weatherworn wood, dead plants, even newspapers) and salivary secretions. This species is also known as an Umbrella Wasp, as its small nest looks like an inside-out umbrella hanging from a thin stalk. Frequently found under eaves or inside attics (nice, dry places), it may have twenty to two hundred open cells that point downward. The nest is often coated with a dark secretion that repels ants, who would otherwise gladly carry off the eggs and larvae.

Northern Paper Wasps are yellow to reddish brown, slightly larger and more slender than yellowjackets, but often confused with them. Both show up at picnic or garbage sites, or on fallen fruit. Females are slow to sting and have short, straight antennae, dark triangular faces, and pointed abdomens; males have long, curled antennae, square yellow faces, and blunt abdomens. The yellow-and-brown-striped body pattern varies by location, and nestmates recognize each individual based on her unique facial and abdominal markings.

WESTERN YELLOWJACKET
(to ⅝ inch long)

Notorious for being combative and often mistaken for hornets or Honey Bees, yellowjackets are sometimes called meat bees (though they are not bees) for their tendency to raid summer picnics and barbecues to feed their young. Western Yellowjackets usually nest underground, often in abandoned rodent burrows, but will also build nests in trees or woodpiles, or occasionally in walls or attics. A mature nest has multiple layers of horizontal paper combs, insulated and protected by additional paperlike layers made from chewed-up wood.

The same size as Honey Bees, Western Yellowjackets are agile, athletic aviators, and sport a striking and distinctive bright yellow-and-black pattern, including yellow eye rings. Without a waggle dance to broadcast the location of resources, each forager is on her own as she searches for honeydew, nectar, water, wood fibers, and prey (caterpillars, flies, mosquitoes, and even slugs).

A colony of a couple thousand workers, larvae, and pupae is a huge protein meal for predators, so yellowjackets aggressively defend their nest. Keep an eye out for a stream of striped traffic entering and exiting the nest through its single, mud-lined opening, and don't step there! Injured and stinging yellow-jackets send alarm signals to their sisters, creating a battalion to assail intruders en masse.

Except in the warmest climates, yellowjacket nests last only a year. At the end of the summer, newly mated queens fly away to hibernate while the remaining workers die or become a zesty meal for moles, raccoons, or skunks.

BALD-FACED HORNET
(to ⅞ inch long)

Beware those common names! The Bald-Faced Hornet is also called the White-Faced Hornet (it has handsome white markings on its face, body, and legs), but it is not a hornet. The only true hornet in North America, the European Hornet, lives mostly on the East Coast.

Resembling true hornets in size and nest type, Bald-Faced Hornets are actually wasps, closely related to yellowjackets. Being kin doesn't ensure good relations; in fact, Bald-Faced Hornets are active predators of yellowjackets—some nests are so packed with remains that they are yellowish inside. Bald-Faced Hornets also prey on flies, spiders, caterpillars, beetles, and other wasps; they rarely scavenge, so you usually won't find these wasps at your barbecue. And despite its scary-large size, a Bald-Faced Hornet is relatively docile unless protecting its nest.

The turnip-shaped nest of a Bald-Faced Hornet colony is large (up to 23 inches long when mature) and closed, composed of several tiers of combs surrounded by layer upon layer of delicate paper with a single entrance at the bottom. Generally hung high up in trees or bushes or on buildings or utility poles, the nest is home to up to seven hundred workers and is a tempting treat to bold squirrels, raccoons, and birds. After the first heavy frost of the year, the hive is probably empty (and will not be used again); it's worth taking it down and peeling off the outer layers to see the beautiful structure of the combs underneath.

— Ants —

Unlike their bee and wasp cousins, all ant species are social. Ants are an incredibly successful group, living on every continent except Antarctica, and making up almost 10 percent of the animal biomass on the planet—in the Amazon rainforest, it's more like a third. An ant colony can thrive for twenty to thirty years, the lifetime of its queen. Complex social organization allows ants to customize their environment, defend the nest, and locate, store, and sometimes even cultivate food. Many species share symbiotic relationships with plants or other animals—usually the ants receive nutrition and provide fierce protection. All ants can bite, and some have stingers.

Like other social insects, ants have a sophisticated system of communication, using pheromones produced in glands all over their bodies—even their feet! Different pheromone combinations are used for recognizing other ants, marking territory, calling for help, advertising the location of a food source, et cetera. Pheromone trails leading to something delicious are followed and reinforced.

ARGENTINE ANT
(to ⅛ inch long)

The ants traipsing into your kitchen or bathroom are likely Argentine Ants (although there are other species that frequent yards and homes). This tiny brown ant was introduced into the United States in the late 1800s by ships from South America, and it has become one of the most invasive species in the world.

A typical insect colony has one queen and fiercely defends its nest against foreign invaders (even insects of the same species); the reproductive ants of most species are winged and go on a special mating flight that's great for genetic diversity but exposes them to predators. A young Argentine Ant queen avoids that threat by mating within the safety of the nest. She then takes a short stroll with a crew of workers to break ground on a new nest, which remains part of her original colony. The result is that many colonies, with multiple queens, can be related and work cooperatively. One "super colony" stretches over five hundred miles along the coast of California!

Argentine Ants nest in cracks in the sidewalk, in the ground, or sometimes inside your home. Even if you have the cleanest house on the block, you may get a visit from ants looking for water (if it's dry out) or shelter (if it's cold or if rain has flooded their nests). Argentine Ants don't sting or carry disease, and they won't harm your house.

Mostly an inconvenience for us, Argentine Ants pose a problem for native ants (which they displace in urban areas) and the plants and animals that rely on them. Argentine Ants find and deplete food sources more quickly than smaller colonies can, and they deal viciously with competitors. Called Sugar Ants in their native Argentina, they prefer sweet food—a major source is honeydew from aphids, scale insects, and the like. The ants help spread these agricultural pests and protect them from their natural predators.

Ants are tasty morsels for spiders, amphibians, reptiles, cockroaches, and some birds.

ARACHNIDS

Spiders, scorpions, ticks, and mites—perhaps more than any group of animals, arachnids give people the heebie-jeebies. Arachnids have no wings or antennae, and they have eight legs, some of which may be modified for different functions. An arachnid's head is a busy place, adorned with two pairs of specialized appendages: jawlike chelicerae for feeding and defense, and pedipalps for eating, walking, and/or mating. Most are predators; some are scavengers or parasites.

The most familiar arachnids are spiders, which have two distinct body parts. The first section (head and thorax fused together) carries eyes (usually eight), sharp chelicerae that can deliver a dose of venom, and hydraulic legs! With flexor muscles but no extensors, a spider extends its legs by forcing blood into each segment, giving it a characteristic creepy walking style. A dehydrated or dead spider's legs can only flex, curling inward.

Using spinnerets on its abdomen, a spider can produce different widths and varieties of silk, wind different types together, or coat the strands with sticky or waterproof substances. Incredibly flexible, and some (like the black widow's) stronger than steel or Kevlar, the silk is used to catch prey, wrap up the meal, form draglines, weave silken cases for eggs, and carry baby spiders along with a breeze. A male spider even uses silk for mating—he has no penis, so he deposits a sperm droplet onto a small "sperm web." He sucks the sperm into his pedipalps and is ready to find a mate.

With a narrow gut and no jaws for chewing, a spider must liquefy its food by grinding it with the bases of its pedipalps or flooding it with digestive enzymes before sucking the juicy feast through a series of filters.

The measurements given below represent the length of the arachnid's body (not including its legs).

BLACK AND YELLOW GARDEN SPIDER
(to 1 ⅛ inches)

This gold, silver, and black stunner is hard to miss, poised in the center of her two-foot web across your garden gate or amongst the plants. One of the orb-weaving spiders, like the impressively literate Charlotte of *Charlotte's Web*, her web is classic Halloween-style with radiating lines connected by an elastic, sticky spiral. The adult adds a zigzag of white silk through the middle of the web; an immature female has striped legs and makes a circular central patch of zigzags. This special silk reflects ultraviolet light more than the rest of the web, possibly mimicking the way flowers reflect UV light to attract insects looking for nectar. What an unpleasant surprise to fly toward a "flower" and get stuck in a web!

Like other web builders, the Black and Yellow Garden Spider's eyesight isn't very sharp—she relies on an incredible sensitivity to smell, vibration, and touch to build her beautiful web

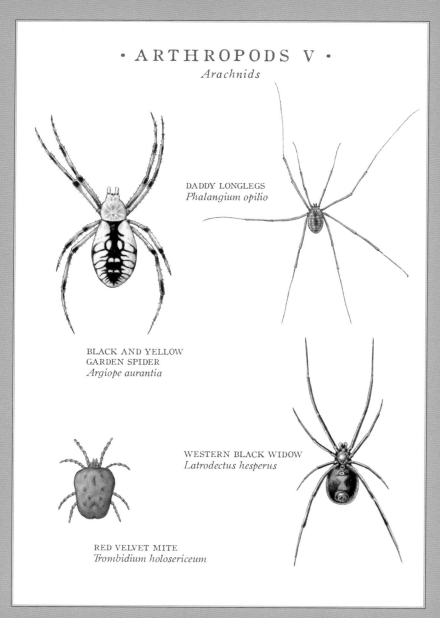

· ARTHROPODS V ·
Arachnids

DADDY LONGLEGS
Phalangium opilio

BLACK AND YELLOW
GARDEN SPIDER
Argiope aurantia

WESTERN BLACK WIDOW
Latrodectus hesperus

RED VELVET MITE
Trombidium holosericeum

and identify visitors. The much smaller (⅜-inch) male plucks on the edges of her web to announce his presence and intention to mate. If an insect has been trapped, she may vigorously shake the web to further ensnare it, or immediately paralyze it with a venomous bite before wrapping it up for later. She does not become stuck herself: she avoids the sticky lines if she can, walks gingerly through them if she must, and employs a nonstick leg coating as a further guarantee.

Most nights she eats her elaborate web and builds a new one over several hours.

WESTERN BLACK WIDOW
(to ½ inch)

You don't have to have arachnophobia to feel uneasy around this glossy black spider with an orange-red hourglass warning mark on her belly. The adult female's venom is up to fifteen times more toxic than a rattlesnake's, but this shy creature would prefer to retreat, only biting if surprised or squeezed—and even then, she delivers a much smaller dose of venom than a snake can. Still, see a doctor if you're bitten.

Cracks, crevices, and cluttered corners around and inside homes are common places for her irregular tangle of webbing built from the strongest silk in the world.

An adult male black widow retains the light brown body, white striping, and light-colored hourglass of juvenile spiders. Once mature, he fills his pedipalps with sperm and goes a-wandering, forsaking food in search of a mate. Only one third her size, he approaches a female with caution, using cues from her appearance and pheromone-infused web to determine whether she is hungry, and then he lets her know he is a male (not lunch) with a special web-vibrating courtship dance. Only rarely does she make herself a true widow by eating her suitor.

One mating can yield several half-inch-long, teardrop-shaped egg sacs, each filled with hundreds of eggs. The young that survive (some cannibalism usually takes place) climb to the top of their mother's web, release a strand or two of silk, and let a passing breeze carry them off.

Three species of black widow live in the United States, as well as a chocolate-colored, European-imported, false (and nonvenomous) black widow that's common inside Pacific coast homes.

DADDY LONGLEGS
(to ⅜ inch)

Have you heard that a daddy longlegs possesses a highly toxic venom, but its fangs are too short to bite a human? First, figure out who you're calling a daddy longlegs. Some people give this moniker to crane flies (insects that can't bite); others ascribe it to the cellar spider, which is commonly found in homes but produces a weak venom. If you're thinking of the garden-dwelling daddy longlegs with a little brown pill of a body, suspended by eight incredibly long and delicate legs, know that this arachnid isn't even a spider! Harvestman is a more specific common name for this little beast.

Daddy longlegs are not true spiders—they do not have two distinct body segments, and they bear only two eyes. With no fangs or venom, their chelicerae are used mostly for grabbing food. They can swallow small chunks of soft insects and other invertebrates, fungi, earthworms, and dead or decaying plants and animals.

Lacking silk glands, a daddy longlegs can't make a web. The male has a penis, so there's no need for a sperm web, and the female tucks her fertilized eggs into damp moss, rotting wood, or moist soil for protection.

Introduced to North America from Europe, daddy longlegs are quite gentle and don't bite, but can give off an unpleasant odor. As most children have discovered, a daddy longlegs occasionally loses a leg or two, which twitches around to distract an attacker. If you'd like to hold one, coax it onto your hand. Notice how it waves its second pair of legs like antennae to investigate its surroundings.

 ### RED VELVET MITE
(to ⅙ inch)

Some of the most diminutive arachnids, mighty mites live everywhere in the world, including Antarctica and the deep ocean. Of the almost fifty thousand species, some are predators, parasites, decomposers, or herbivores; most are microscopic. Red velvet mites, with species numbering in the thousands, are all shockingly bright red from the center of the fuzzy body to the tips of their eight legs, and they're often seen swarming sidewalks or porches after rain or a lawn watering.

The complex life cycle of the urban red velvet mite includes a six-legged larva that parasitizes insects and spiders; as adults they inhabit the soil and prey on small invertebrates and their eggs.

While these mites are large (for mites), they are no match for the related Giant Red Velvet Mites of the American Southwest and India, which can be up to half an inch long.

AMPHIBIANS

Frogs, toads, and salamanders come in a rainbow of colors and lifestyles, but all retain close ties to water. They don't drink, and their lungs (which only some amphibians possess) are primitive—they rely on thin, permeable skin to absorb oxygen and water. Some produce smelly or mildly toxic substances to discourage predators. Handle only with clean and gentle hands, and make sure to wash thoroughly afterwards.

Mucus glands help keep their delicate skin moist, but most amphibians also need damp environments. Even the toad (a type of frog, which is terrestrial, usually with dry, bumpy skin) starts life in the water. Sometimes in great numbers, amphibians converge at bodies of water in the spring. Once they pair up, the male grasps the female with his front legs, and sheds sperm over the jelly-covered eggs she lays in the water. Gilled, swimming larvae (like tadpoles) hatch and feed until they undergo metamorphosis, transforming into air-breathing, land-loving adults.

Reliance on water, a complex life cycle, and permeable skin and eggs make amphibians particularly vulnerable to UV radiation, pathogens, and chemical contamination: amphibian populations are good indicators of the health of an environment.

PACIFIC TREEFROG
(to 2 inches)

If a nighttime scene in a movie has atmospheric croaking in the background, it's likely the call of this splendid little frog, also called the Pacific Chorus Frog. Hundreds of males congregate near ponds during breeding season and sing loudly to attract females. They trill day and night when temperature and humidity are just right. It's a common night sound on the West Coast, so easy to record in Hollywood that it became a standard sound effect long ago, even for movies that take place far from the frog's natural range.

A Pacific Treefrog is loud but tiny, with a distinctive dark stripe through each glittering bronze eye, and large sticky toe pads to help it climb on shrubs and grasses. A tasty mouthful for larger frogs, snakes, raccoons, opossums, and birds, the treefrog relies on damp hiding spots and camouflage for protection. Its body may be light yellow green to dark olive brown, and almost anything in between, and it can change from dark to light within a few minutes, in response to temperature, season, and humidity.

After choosing a particularly sweet crooner and laying several hundred eggs in small clusters attached to sticks or stems in ponds or puddles, a female Pacific Treefrog hops away, her duties done; her movie star mate hops back into the throng for another chance to breed.

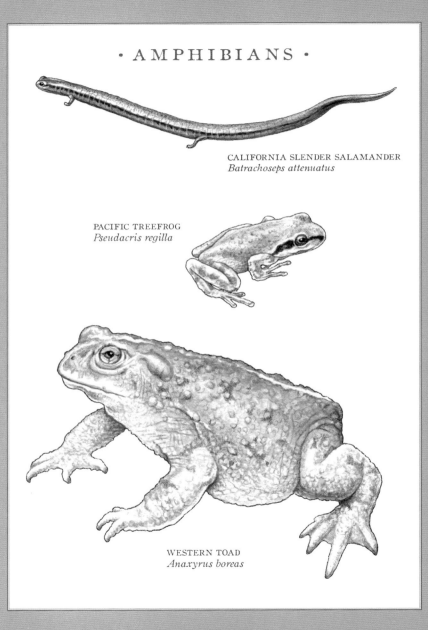

· AMPHIBIANS ·

CALIFORNIA SLENDER SALAMANDER
Batrachoseps attenuatus

PACIFIC TREEFROG
Pseudacris regilla

WESTERN TOAD
Anaxyrus boreas

WESTERN TOAD
(to 5 inches)

Instead of the loud, sonorous ribbit you'd expect, this robust, warty toad emits a chick-like chirp! It's a warning to keep competitors out of its space in a crowded breeding pond.

Aside from its surprisingly dainty voice, a Western Toad is distinguished by horizontal pupils and a pale stripe down the center of its back. Behind each eye lies a swollen bump, the parotid gland, which produces a slightly toxic substance—enough to deter some predators, though not all. Clever ravens have learned to avoid the glands, approaching the delectable innards through the toad's stomach. By the way, you can't get warts from a toad—those are caused by a human virus.

Western Toads can survive in a wide variety of habitats, even deserts, as long as there is a bit of water nearby (even a roadside puddle will do). With long strides and the occasional hop, they are able to cover quite a bit of ground. Toads emerge from hibernation and migrate to spring breeding pools, where each female lays between three thousand and sixteen thousand eggs in long, jellylike strands. Then it's off to foraging grounds, often a mile or more away, where they hunt for invertebrate prey at night. In the fall, toads return to hibernation sites; they can dig their own tunnels but prefer the convenience of ready-made burrows or crevices. They're willing to share, within reason: several toads will often overwinter in the same burrow, as long as everyone has some elbow room. Toads frequently return to the same pond year after year, where their tadpoles swim and feed together. After the springtime metamorphosis, a frenzy of hundreds of thousands of half-inch-long toadlets hop along the border of their natal pond. Some stay close by for their first year, while others venture out in droves.

CALIFORNIA SLENDER SALAMANDER
(to 5 ½ inches, including tail)

If you spy a dark "worm" with a distinct head and eyes and a reddish or brown back, chances are it's a California Slender Salamander. Look closely to see the short, spindly legs. They *can* walk with those little things, but they make more progress using a snakelike wriggle.

Unlike many amphibians, the slender salamander doesn't have an aquatic tadpole. Instead, eggs are laid in the adults' moist habitat—under boards and rocks or in leaf litter—and full development occurs inside the egg, which hatches a teensy salamander. Never growing larger in diameter than a pencil, these salamanders have tiny territories to match—usually no more than six feet across.

Slender salamanders rely on dusky coloration to hide from both predators and prey (small beetles, snails, mites, pillbugs, and other minute invertebrates). When attacked, a salamander thrashes wildly, bouncing to a new spot where it freezes to avoid detection; if necessary, its tail can detach and squirm around as a distraction, and the salamander will eventually grow a new tail.

REPTILES

Slow turtles, zippy lizards, multicolored snakes, 20-foot-long saltwater crocodiles, and 150-year-old tortoises are all reptiles. Unlike amphibians, they are fully adapted to life on land. Even sea turtles are descended from terrestrial ancestors, so they return to land to lay eggs. A reptile's tough, breathable eggshell keeps the developing embryo safe in its own little pond. Dry (not slimy!) skin with overlapping scales protects against damage and water loss, but isn't breathable (reptiles get oxygen from their lungs), and doesn't stretch, so it needs to be shed periodically. A lizard sloughs its skin off in pieces; a snake sheds the whole thing at one time, often pulling the old skin inside out in the process, revealing fresh new scales and leaving behind a ghostly version of itself.

Reptiles aren't "cold-blooded," but ectothermic: their body temperature depends on the environment, and is adjusted by basking in the sun or seeking shade. It might be a little sluggish in cool weather, but by using solar power instead of generating its own body heat, a reptile uses only 5 to 20 percent of the calories that a similar-sized mammal needs to survive. They

· REPTILES ·

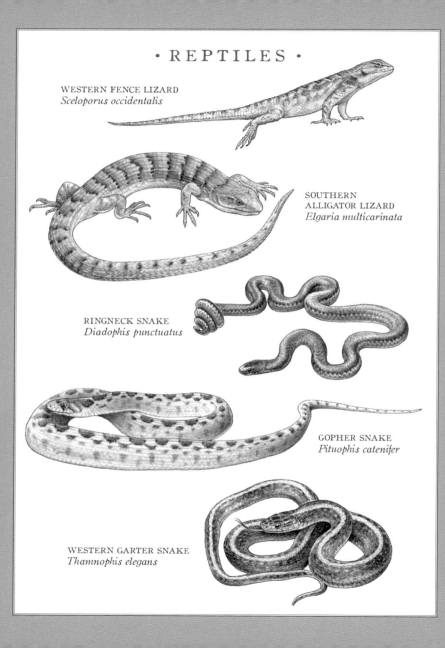

WESTERN FENCE LIZARD
Sceloporus occidentalis

SOUTHERN ALLIGATOR LIZARD
Elgaria multicarinata

RINGNECK SNAKE
Diadophis punctuatus

GOPHER SNAKE
Pituophis catenifer

WESTERN GARTER SNAKE
Thamnophis elegans

don't need to spend as much time searching for food, so can use more energy for growth and reproduction.

Lizards come in all shapes and sizes, many small enough to be delicious tidbits for other reptiles, birds, and mammals. When camouflage and speed fail, some lizards can drop their tail—it detaches and thrashes around, distracting the predator while the lizard scurries away. Over several weeks, a new, less flexible tail grows, restoring the lizard's balance. Several fracture points along the tail allow it to be lost more than once (as long as it's not the whole thing), but it requires a lot of energy to grow a new tail, so dropping a tail is a desperate measure.

Snakes are truly fascinating—imagine trying to travel, hunt, and eat with no hands or legs! Incredibly flexible, muscular bodies with tread-like belly scales give them a wide range of motion for traversing sand, digging through soil, swimming, or even climbing trees. Exquisitely sensitive to scent, heat (in the case of pit vipers like rattlesnakes), and vibration, a snake hones in on its prey. Having no ears or eardrums, the snake picks up on sounds and ground vibrations through its skull, jawbones, and special sense organs throughout its long body. Depending on the species, the snake constricts the prey, strikes and subdues it with venom, or simply swallows it. You can't eat a pizza without cutting it into pieces, but a snake can expand its extremely flexible jaws to engulf a meal larger than its own head.

A tongue-flicking reptile is not trying to lick or sting—many lizards and most snakes smell with their noses *and* tongues! The forked tongue collects particles from the ground and air and delivers them through two little pits on the roof of the mouth to the Jacobson's organ, giving the reptile a stereo sense of smell. The differing number of scent molecules picked up on each side determines the direction so precisely that a snake or lizard is able to follow the trail of prey or a potential mate.

The snakes described below may void musk and excrement or even bite if threatened, but are not dangerous. There are a number of species and subspecies of each of these snakes and lizards, so you may observe slightly different patterns or colors, but their habits are similar.

GARTER SNAKE
(18–50 inches long)

Before socks were elasticized, men used to wear garters to keep them from slipping down. Often striped and colorful, these little belts gave this common suburban and rural snake its name. Red, gray, green, black, or brown, with spots or checkered patterns—such incredible variety, even within the same species, makes garter snakes difficult to identify. Western species usually have a white, yellow, or orange stripe along their back, flanked by a pale stripe along each side. You'll see them flash by when startled, a tail disappearing into the grass.

These slim, graceful snakes are not picky eaters; they are happy to eat slugs, snails, earthworms, lizards, and small mammals in the garden. Populations that live near water are strong swimmers and catch tadpoles, leeches, and fishes. Garter snake saliva contains a mild venom, enough to stun small prey but only to irritate humans.

A female garter snake does not lay eggs, instead retaining them in her body and giving birth to as few as three or as many as eighty snakelets.

GOPHER SNAKE
(2 ½–9 feet long)

When this large, handsome snake is agitated, it hisses

loudly, flattens its oval-shaped head to appear triangular, and rapidly vibrates its tail. It's a respectable enough rattlesnake imitation to scare off some animals but also to get it killed by people afraid of a dangerous snake.

Actually harmless to humans, a Gopher Snake can bite, but has no fangs or venom like the rattlesnake it mimics. Instead, the Gopher Snake is a powerful constrictor—it wraps its coils around prey and squeezes tightly. Constriction doesn't suffocate the quarry, which would take several minutes. Rather, the pressure blocks blood flow, cutting off oxygen to the heart and brain and killing the animal within seconds. Birds and lizards are occasional meals, but rodents (like gophers!) are the Gopher Snake's specialty. An accomplished digger (using its head), this snake won't hesitate to follow them into their burrows.

Sun-loving Gopher Snakes often encounter people (and, sadly, cars) due to their habit of stretching their long bodies full length along trails and roads.

RINGNECK SNAKE
(8–30 inches long)

This beautiful, smooth, and delicate snake is dark gray or olive with a slender ring of bright yellow to orange around its neck. When disturbed, it coils its tail into a corkscrew, revealing a bright orange or red, sometimes speckled, belly. Small and nonaggressive, this warning and a smelly saliva are its main defenses.

Slim as a pencil, the Ringneck Snake eats similarly-shaped slender salamanders, worms, baby snakes, and slugs, as well as small frogs and insects. Hunting by night, it uses constriction and a mild venom to subdue prey. Ringnecks keep a low profile in the day, hiding under wood or stones where the ground is damp.

WESTERN FENCE LIZARD
(to 8 inches, including tail)

This spiny little lizard is one of the most familiar in western states, basking on fence posts, rocks, or piles of wood. Males seek out territories with high perches where they can check out mates and rivals, while performing head bobs and push-ups that show off their brilliant blue sides and throat patches and yellow thighs. Females and juveniles are less colorful. Called Blue-Bellies for their appearance, Western Fence Lizards' darting and dashing also earns them the common name swift. Fence lizards are a crucial part of the food chain, consuming many insects, spiders, and other arthropods, and becoming dinner themselves for almost any snake, bird, or mammal (their penchant for tall posts makes them tempting targets).

Like many lizards, the Western Fence Lizard has a light-sensitive third "eye" on the top of its head that communicates light levels and position of the sun for temperature regulation and navigational purposes. When it's cool, the lizard's scales darken to absorb more warmth; rising temperature causes the scales to lighten and reflect the heat. If it's extremely hot or cold, the lizard will find shelter in a crevice or burrow.

Western Black-Legged Ticks (deer ticks) are frequent carriers of the bacterium that causes Lyme disease, and the nymphs love to feed on lizards. Western Fence Lizard blood contains a protein that kills the bacterium, preventing the lizard from contracting Lyme disease but also killing the bacteria inside the tick, rendering it unable to transmit the disease.

ALLIGATOR LIZARD
(to 16 inches, including tail)

An alligator has armor-like bony plates underneath the scales on its back; the alligator lizard has similar plates on its back and belly. These make the body tough, but rather stiff, so along each side is a lengthwise fold of small, flexible scales to give the lizard some breathing room, as well as space for a big meal or a female's eggs.

With a tail that can be twice the length of its elongate body, and a slightly forked tongue, an alligator lizard looks more like a snake than an alligator, and it often moves like one, tucking its front legs up and undulating for a rapid escape, or slithering into a crevice or rodent burrow, looking for lunch. Any small invertebrate, lizard, or mammal is on the menu. Alligator lizards are excellent swimmers and climbers, and occasionally will dine on bird eggs or baby birds.

Alligator lizards are fairly secretive, hiding under rocks, wood, or vegetation, except when foraging at dawn and dusk. But if under attack, a feisty alligator lizard fights back, showing its teeth and snapping. It will even bite a snake's head and hold on, so the snake can't strike. A male uses this same technique when courting—he will hold the female's head, often for hours, until she is ready to mate.

BIRDS

Whether you live in a country cottage or an urban high-rise, birds are in your neighborhood. A tray or tube of seeds will bring many right to your door if they're not already nesting nearby. Besides enjoying their lovely colors and (mostly) beautiful songs, there's so much to watch—social interactions, territorial behavior (even at the feeder!), how and what they eat, courtship rituals (including singing and offering nesting materials), nest-building, and feeding the young.

Unique to birds (and their extinct relatives, dinosaurs), feathers come in a remarkable array of hues and textures. Feathers help birds camouflage themselves or show off their beauty, but they're not just for looks. Composed of keratin, the wonder protein that forms bird beaks and claws, reptile scales, and our own skin, hair, and nails, feathers shed water and provide insulation to keep body temperature stable—and, of course, they facilitate birds' marvelous ability to fly. Feathers are key to survival, so a bird takes great care to groom and clean itself, applying a conditioning secretion from a gland near its tail, and bathing in water or dust to keep its plumes in tip-top shape.

A feather that is accidentally lost grows back, and each year (often in the fall), all the feathers are shed and replaced with a fresh new set.

Powered flight requires a combination of strength and minimal weight. So a bird's anatomy is streamlined—a beak instead of a toothed jaw; bones honeycombed with air spaces; and only one functional ovary and oviduct in females of most species. Birds don't even have bladders! Humans excrete urea, which needs to be diluted in water, but water is precious, and heavy, so birds excrete uric acid as a pasty white goo, along with dark feces.

The energy and oxygen demands of flight are considerable compared to running or walking. A bird is graced with a large and mighty heart, a fascinating respiratory system that supplies the lungs with fresh air during inhalation *and* exhalation, and an efficient, highly specialized digestive system. Some species have a pouch-like crop in the esophagus where food can be stored, allowing them to quickly shovel in a meal and digest it later in a safe place. Having no teeth, birds cannot chew. Food passes through one stomach with digestive enzymes (much like ours), then continues into a muscular gizzard to be pulverized (the job of our teeth). Seed- and nut-eating birds consume small stones and other grit, which collect in the gizzard, to help crush their hard-hulled snacks.

Bird diets depend on the season—birds known as seed eaters will also dine on plentiful spring and summer insects, and feed them to their ravenous young, who need the protein. Fruits and berries are often available later in the year. Species that are purely insectivorous are likely to migrate, following their prey to warmer climes.

Incredibly, birds can navigate across counties or countries using the earth's magnetic field and the location of the sun, stars, and other landmarks, but it's difficult for one to find its

ANNA'S HUMMINGBIRD
Calypte anna

MOURNING DOVE
Zenaida macroura

HOUSE FINCH
Carpodacus mexicanus

ROCK PIGEON
Columba livia

HOUSE SPARROW
Passer domesticus

STELLER'S JAY
Cyanocitta stelleri

BREWER'S BLACKBIRD
Euphagus cyanocephalus

AMERICAN CROW
Corvus brachyrhynchos

AMERICAN ROBIN
Turdus migratorius

· BIRDS ·

NORTHERN MOCKINGBIRD
Mimus polyglottos

DARK-EYED JUNCO
Junco hyemalis

EUROPEAN STARLING
Sternus vulgaris

WHITE-CROWNED SPARROW
Zonotrichia leucophrys

CALIFORNIA SCRUB-JAY
Aphelocoma californica

COMMON RAVEN
Corvus corax

way out of your house. A bird's instinct is to fly up when flustered, so if necessary, toss a towel over the bird, carefully gather it up, and release it outdoors. A towel is too heavy for a hummingbird—try tempting it with a hummingbird feeder (or anything red) at the exit; if it lands inside, pick it up very gently and place it outside in a safe, shady spot.

A baby bird that has fallen from its nest can be returned—its parents will care for it, although it might take time before they feel comfortable returning to the nest after seeing (big, scary) you. If the baby has feathers and small wings and is hopping around uninjured, leave it alone—many birds leave the nest a few days before they can fly: their parents feed and protect them while they learn to fly, find food, and recognize predators.

Most songbirds always appear to be on edge—all stages of their life cycle are tasty treats for any number of mammals, reptiles, and even other birds. Excellent hearing and vision help them stay safe—many birds can sleep with one eye open and one half of the brain awake! Many birds also form flocks after the nesting season, gaining safety in numbers to better find food and detect predators.

This chapter contains a sampling of some of the most common backyard songbirds. If you are particularly smitten with our high-performance feathered friends, it might be worth investing in a dedicated bird guide and a pair of binoculars.

The sizes listed below reflect the average length of the bird from bill tip to tail tip.

ROCK PIGEON
(12 ½ inches)

Often overlooked or despised as "rats with wings," hardy, admirable pigeons share a rich history with humans. Domesticated for at least five thousand years (they appear in Egyptian hieroglyphics), and brought to North America by European settlers in the 1600s, they have been used as food, bred for fancy colors and patterns, and trained as homing and carrier pigeons. The strong, fast fliers carried messages in ancient Rome, during the Napoleonic Wars and the two world wars.

Urban pigeons have swapped cliffside nest sites for artificial ones (high window ledges, bridges, lofty construction sites, et cetera), and seeds for bread crumbs and trash. Since they hang out in flocks near people, they are easy to observe. Check out their surprisingly bright-orange eyes! If you study a few flocks, you'll find that some have white eyes and that young pigeons' eyes are dark. The pigeon depicted shows the bluish-gray plumage most similar to its wild ancestors'; many other colors and patterns, from pure white to mottled red or black, are left over from selective breeding by pigeon fanciers. Watch for courtship displays—a male puffs up his lovely iridescent neck feathers, bows, coos, and struts around a female (usually smaller, with less iridescence).

Rock Pigeons mate for life, with occasional dalliances. In addition to sharing nest-building and egg-sitting duties, both parents secrete and regurgitate a yellowish, curd-like "pigeon milk" from their crops. Similar to mammals' milk, it's high in protein, fat, antibodies, and immune-system boosters—the perfect first food for growing pigeons. After a few days, seeds are added to the milk, and finally the young are weaned.

Big-city pigeons often have rather unappealing feet—one or both may be deformed, missing toes, or absent altogether. Infection or disease can be the culprit, but usually filamentous garbage (human hair, fishing line, thread, and the like) catches in the foot scales, becomes entangled, and cuts off circulation. Ouch! Collateral damage from their close ties to people.

MOURNING DOVE
(12 inches)

The plaintive "ooOOO-ooo-ooo-ooo" from dawn to dusk is not an owl but our native Mourning Dove. They differ from Rock Pigeons in their smaller size, dark eyes, soft gray-brown coloration, and habit of hanging out in pairs or small groups while searching for seeds. The two *are* closely related—larger species in the family are called pigeons, smaller ones doves—and Mourning Doves share the key traits of Rock Pigeons discussed above. But while baby pigeons are rarely seen, young Mourning Doves might be right outside your kitchen window! Instead of nesting high and out of sight, Mourning Doves assemble flimsy nests in trees, hanging baskets, eaves, or rain gutters. And they are prolific—in warm climes they may raise up to six pairs of eggs in one year.

Listen for the twittery whistling sound made by a Mourning Dove's wings during takeoff and landing. It may startle predators or alert flock mates to potential danger; the dove can also make a quieter clapping sound as it lifts off.

ANNA'S HUMMINGBIRD
(4 inches)

Zippy, buzzy hummingbirds are the glittering jewels of the garden. With his noisy chattering, vivid green-bronze feathers, brilliantly iridescent rose-red head, and feisty attitude, a male Anna's Hummingbird is hard to miss, even though he's only a few inches long and weighs about as much as a nickel. The structure of his feathers refracts sunlight like a prism, causing iridescence. If the sun isn't hitting at the right angle, the feathers appear dark and allow him to be more camouflaged.

The female's appearance is more subdued, though a few sparkly red feathers often decorate her throat. The male strives to impress her with a spectacular dive display (also used to aggressively protect territory from other birds, or people). Always angled so the sun reflects his fabulous colors in her direction, he hovers in front of her and sings, flies straight up twelve stories into the air, then rapidly plummets (at up to sixty miles per hour!), breaking his fall with a dramatic swoop that vibrates his tail feathers like a clarinet reed, creating a loud chirp, just above the female. If you miss it the first time, don't worry—he often repeats the display several times to make his point.

After all that attention, the female is on her own when it comes to raising her young. She builds a compact, walnut-sized nest of plant fibers and spiderwebs, camouflaged with lichens and mosses, and lays two pinto-bean-sized white eggs.

Wings ablur, whizzing up to ninety times a second, a hummingbird can fly forward, backward, and briefly, upside down; it can even hover. Its heart beats over 1,200 times per minute and its body temperature is over 100 degrees Fahrenheit—such a breakneck metabolism requires a lot of fuel. Always just hours from starvation, a hummingbird visits (and pollinates) hundreds of flowers every day, preferably pink, red, orange, or purple tube-shaped blooms. A long, forked tongue flicks in and out fifteen to twenty times per second, unfurling lengthwise to draw in the liquid goodness. Tree sap, small insects and spiders (for protein and fat), and hummingbird feeders also provide nutrition (keep your feeder clean and fresh, with only pure sugar, please).

On cold nights, a hummingbird cannot maintain its high body temperature and goes into a hibernation-like torpor, markedly slowing its metabolism, dropping its body temperature by half, and becoming completely immobile. As the air temperature warms in the morning, it takes about twenty minutes for the bird to rev up its engine before it can fly off for breakfast.

A hummingbird is so well adapted for flying that its flight muscles make up over a quarter of its body weight (for other birds it's closer to 15 percent). Small, weak legs and feet allow the bird to perch, scoot along a branch, and groom itself, but not to walk or hop.

CALIFORNIA SCRUB-JAY
(11 inches)

This vibrantly colored, brash, and sassy bird is *a* blue jay, but not *the* Blue Jay, which occurs in Midwestern and eastern states. All seemingly blue feathers are actually brown! Hold one up so light shines *through* it to see this. If light shines *on* a feather, microscopic air pockets in the fibers scatter and reflect blue wavelengths of light, much in the way gas molecules in the atmosphere scatter blue light, making the sky appear blue.

Jays and their relatives, crows and ravens, are loud, bold, curious, and exceptionally intelligent. Jays typically mate for life (unless someone else has a particularly fabulous territory or is a superior parent), keeping close tabs on each other and sharing nest-building duties and all aspects of parenting. They serenade each other with a sweetness that contrasts with the harsh, scolding squawks the rest of us hear—they seem to enjoy mobbing and taunting anyone who stumbles onto their turf.

STELLER'S JAY
(11 ½ inches)

With its rich deep-blue body, dark shoulders, black head, and jaunty crest, it's easy to tell a Steller's Jay from a California Scrub-Jay. Its voice is a bit more raspy, and it tends to prefer more forested environs, but it otherwise shares much with its relative: a confident manner, omnivorous ways, gender equality, and shrewd slyness. Besides keeping track of hundreds to thousands of its own stashed acorns, a jay will observe and then steal other birds' hidden caches, or even their eggs or young. In social groups or on its own, this bright and inquisitive jay notices and investigates anything new, reporting it all with a wide repertoire of noisy calls and notes.

AMERICAN CROW
(17 ½ inches)

Common throughout much of the United States, American Crows are large, lustrous black birds with a raucous "caw!" and a swagger in their step. Too smart to be scared of scarecrows, these brainy, playful birds are quick learners and excellent problem solvers. They have been known to use tools, and they sometimes work in pairs to distract and steal meals from other animals, or in gangs to mob predators. They mate for life, and young crows often stay with their parents for a few years, helping defend territory, scout out food, and raise younger siblings. In the fall and winter, crows may assemble by the thousands to roost and forage. A gathering is called a murder of crows, a nod to their sinister reputation, likely stemming from old superstitions based on their dark color and scavenging habits. They actually eat most anything, from roadkill, small animals, insects, and eggs to nuts, seeds, and garbage.

COMMON RAVEN
(24 inches)

Ravens are often confused with crows, and for good reason—both are sizable, intelligent, all-black birds with presence and attitude. A raven is a more massive bird, with a longer, stouter bill, and a ruff of neck feathers. Look for a wedge-shaped tail in flight, compared with a crow's fan-shaped tail. Young ravens sometimes hang out in lively flocks, but adults often travel alone or in pairs. Additionally, a raven has a low, croaking voice that is utterly distinctive. It produces a large variety of vocalizations and can mimic the sounds of other animals, including human speech.

Adaptable and omnivorous, able to survive in the desert or the Arctic tundra, and with few predators due to its large size and quick wits, a raven struts around confidently, like it owns the place.

AMERICAN ROBIN
(10 inches)

The classic harbinger of spring, the early bird catching the worm with a loud, cheerful morning melody, the American Robin is probably the most familiar neighborhood bird. It has a rusty red chest and belly and a sunny yellow bill and acts as perky as it looks, hopping around the yard and stopping to cock its head as it watches for slight movements that could signal a juicy worm or tasty insect. "Robin's-egg blue" is an official color! The actual eggs range from white to blue or blue-green.

A male makes himself conspicuous in the spring when he establishes a territory and tries to lure a mate with his dashing good looks and lovely song, though he may not have been far away during the winter: many robins don't migrate much, but spend less time in our yards in the cooler months as they roost in trees and search for fruits and berries.

NORTHERN MOCKINGBIRD
(10 inches)

Far from bashful, a Northern Mockingbird perches up high, showing off his dashing gray-and-black plumage and singing a loud and astonishing variety of songs, calls, and imitations of anything he has heard: other birds' songs, squeaky screen doors, dog barks, sirens, squirrels—you name it! He flashes white wing and tail patches and flits down to look for insects or chase intruders from his territory. Becoming especially aggressive once he has young to protect, he doesn't hesitate to challenge any predator—cat, snake, owl, or human.

Female mockingbirds sing mostly in the fall, probably to claim territories. It's the males who sing for hours during the day, and bachelor males who continue to sing well into the night. Pop in your earplugs, or just enjoy the concert.

EUROPEAN STARLING
(8 ½ inches)

Back in 1890, it seemed like a good idea to release European Starlings in New York City, in an attempt to introduce all the species of birds mentioned in Shakespeare's plays. Most introductions were unsuccessful, but the starling population exploded. Thriving in various habitats, and not picky about their meals, starlings quickly spread across the country, ravaging crops and frustrating people with their large, noisy, messy roosts. Native bird species barely stand a chance when a large flock of starlings descends on a food source, and starlings aggressively steal nesting sites as well.

Stocky-bodied European Starlings have a waddling gait and brilliant plumage—in the autumn, the pale tips of their dark feathers glow like little stars in the night sky; by spring, the feather tips have worn away, leaving the birds a glistening black, with green and purple iridescence. To top off the effect, fall's dull-brownish bill changes to bright yellow in the spring, in striking contrast to the base of the bill, which is blue in males and pink in females.

A group of starlings is called a murmuration, as is the breathtaking phenomenon of hundreds or thousands of starlings swooping and swirling across the sky in a mesmerizing, pulsating cloud.

WHITE-CROWNED SPARROW
(7 inches)

There are at least thirty-five sparrows native to North America, many of which, to the casual observer, look similar. The White-Crowned Sparrow is one of the easiest to identify, with tidy black and white stripes on its head (juveniles' stripes are brown and tan). White-Crowned Sparrows are common at backyard feeders, especially on the ground, where they prefer to forage. Watch for "double scratching," a quick back-and-forth hop to uncover seeds or insects (which the stout, conical bill is perfect for handling). A short, sweet whistling song ends in a trill, and each population has its own variation.

Populations of White-Crowned Sparrows make appearances in all states at some point during annual migrations, while the Pacific coast harbors year-round residents.

DARK-EYED JUNCO
(6 ¼ inches)

The Dark-Eyed Junco is a common sparrow across the United States, but you might need help from a birder to recognize them all as the same species—depending on the region, they can be dark gray, light gray, or brown. Some have a rusty back patch, while others have a gray or charcoal hood. All have flashy white tail feathers seen in displays and during flight. Illustrated is the "Oregon" subspecies. Dark-Eyed Juncos are seed- and insect-eating ground feeders, like the White-Crowned Sparrow, so you may see them below your feeder. They typically have a pecking order, with older males and earlier arrivals closer to the top—look for aggressive displays and lunges to see who gets to eat first.

BREWER'S BLACKBIRD
(9 inches)

Slim, long-legged Brewer's Blackbird males are resplendent, glossy black birds with gleaming blue, green, and violet iridescence, made even more stunning by their pale yellow eyes. The females have a pleasant, more quiet beauty, in shades of brown with dark eyes. Juvenile males look much like females, but with yellow eyes. These social birds have adapted well to human civilization, and are just as comfortable in agricultural fields or outside a café as they are in woods or meadows. Also look for them perching high up in trees or on power lines, often in flocks with other black birds, including European Starlings.

HOUSE FINCH
(6 inches)

House Finches, with their cheerful songs and hues, are native to the American Southwest, but became part of an underground, illegal pet trade in the early 1900s. Renamed Hollywood Finches, they were shipped by the thousands to the East Coast and sold as exotic pets. When authorities were alerted in 1940, New York City dealers released their birds to escape prosecution. The highly social little birds proved surprisingly adaptable, not only establishing nesting colonies in the area, but expanding across the continent, meeting up with their native range within fifty years.

A male House Finch's face, chest, and rump may be bright red, or occasionally orange or yellow, depending on his diet. The grayish-brown females tend to prefer the reddest males, especially in their first year of breeding. As their name implies, House Finches often nest in shrubbery, eaves, ventholes, or other nooks and crannies near homes, and are frequent visitors to bird feeders.

HOUSE SPARROW
(6 ¼ inches)

In the mid–1800s, many types of European songbirds were released in American cities (remember the starlings?), in some cases to remind immigrants from Europe of their homeland, in others to attempt to control insect pests. Most birds perished quickly, but House Sparrows found plenty to eat (alas, they ate more seeds and grain than insects), aggressively pushed out native bird species, and prospered in their new home—so much so, that by the 1870s, some states unsuccessfully tried to eradicate them during the "Sparrow Wars" —a few even offered a bounty for each bird outlaw collected.

Traveling by wing, in grain boxcars, and with bird lovers; willing to nest just about anywhere near people (in signs, drainpipes, streetlights, other birds' nests); growing quickly, and reproducing like crazy (up to twenty chicks per season), House Sparrows are now one of our most abundant songbirds. They are quite handsome—a breeding male sports a gray cap and crisp chestnut, white, and black markings, including a black bib that indicates his place in the pecking order. The female has black and brown streaks on her back and wings, and subtle brown-toned facial stripes. Listen for flocks singing in the trees or squabbling over food at the feeder.

MAMMALS

Mammals include majestic whales, flying bats, climbing squirrels, burrowing moles, predatory lions, herbivorous cows, and us! Being warm-blooded, mammals can stay active in all climates, but it requires a great deal of energy. Highly specialized teeth grind, shear, crush, or pierce, allowing mammals to take best advantage of the fuel at hand. Hair helps with insulation and can work as camouflage or waterproofing, or for communication (think of a dog raising its hackles or a deer flashing its white tail to signal alarm).

Most mammals bear live young, avoiding the risks of their eggs being eaten; then they nurse and care for their young, protecting them while teaching important survival skills.

The largest mammal group is rodents—mice, rats, squirrels, and their kin. Self-sharpening front teeth are handy for chewing on tough roots, nuts, and seeds, but those teeth are ever-growing, so rodents must constantly gnaw to keep them trim—if not on food, then on wood or your electrical wiring (squirrel teeth grow about six inches in a year, so it's no wonder they do so much damage). While bothersome in our homes, crop fields, or food stores, in nature rodents are beneficial consumers of weed seeds and insects, and they are an important source of food for predators.

Have you ever seen a raccoon or cat's eyes glowing in the night? Many nocturnal animals, and those active at dawn and dusk, have a pearly, mirrorlike layer of tissue called a tapetum lucidum behind the retina (the light-sensitive "movie screen" at the back of the eye that sends images to the brain). Light comes into the eye, passes through the retina, hits the tapetum lucidum, and is reflected back through the retina, improving the animal's night vision and appearing to us as eyeshine.

Some mammals are carriers of the rabies virus. Stay away and alert animal control if you see an animal looking ill, ungroomed, and disoriented. Female raccoons and skunks will forage in the daytime to secure the extra food needed for their young, so unusual hours are not enough of an indicator.

The measurements given below reflect the maximum length of an animal's head and body.

VIRGINIA OPOSSUM
(to 20 inches)

Opossums are hands-down the oddest mammal you'll see trotting across the yard at night. Often mistaken for giant rats, they are the only marsupial (bearing a pouch, like kangaroos) native to the United States. A long, hairless, prehensile tail adds stability while climbing trees and fences, and opossums can even use it to carry nesting material. The babies can hang by their tails, but not for very long, and adults are too big to give it a go. Climbing is assisted by hind feet that grasp like hands, with clawless, opposable thumbs. Fifty teeth make

101

· MAMMALS ·

VIRGINIA OPOSSUM
Didelphis marsupialis

EASTERN GRAY SQUIRREL
Sciurus carolinensis

HOUSE MOUSE
Mus musculus

NORTHERN RACCOON
Procyon lotor

BOTTA'S POCKET GOPHER
Thomomys bottae

NORWAY RAT
Rattus norvegicus

STRIPED SKUNK
Mephitis mephitis

CALIFORNIA VOLE
Microtus californicus

BROAD-FOOTED MOLE
Scapanus latimanus

them the toothiest land animal, and they keep themselves scrupulously clean—reducing tick populations by killing nearly all ticks found while grooming. Opossums are resistant to rabies and immune to the venom of snakes, scorpions, and Honey Bees, as well as to some plant and bacterial toxins. An opossum will happily chow down on a rattlesnake!

Unfairly, opossums are famous not for these superpowers, but for "playing possum." Slow, shy, and gentle, they have few defenses against predators like hawks, owls, coyotes, bobcats, and dogs. A threatened opossum hisses, displaying its many teeth, and tries to run away; if cornered, it involuntarily falls unconscious—mouth open and drooling, body stiff and unresponsive, sometimes releasing a stinky green fluid from glands near the tail. Some predators lose interest when their quarry looks dead, some don't.

The omnivorous opossum's diet includes truly everything: insects, worms, rats, snakes, birds, fruits, vegetables—even pet food and carrion. Sniffing along roads looking for, or eating, animals hit by cars, opossums often become roadkill themselves. They rarely live longer than two years.

Native to warm, southeastern states, opossums were introduced west of the Rockies multiple times around the turn of the century as culinary delicacies, exotic pets, and sources of fur. The shelter of our homes and structures (in addition to abandoned burrows and hollow logs) has allowed them to flourish and spread where it's not too cold or dry.

Mature by eight months, a female may raise up to three litters a year. After a short gestation period (about twelve days), between eight and sixteen pink, Honey Bee–sized babies (called joeys, just like their kangaroo cousins) are born hairless, blind, and deaf with unformed, paddle-like hind limbs. The only developed features are muscular front legs for crawling from the mother's abdomen to her fur-lined pouch; large, open nostrils for navigation; and an open mouth to latch on to one of the thirteen nipples for the next two months (extra babies are out of luck). Once a young opossum has matured enough to detach, it climbs out and clings to its mother's back when the pouch is too crowded.

Early European settlers thought opossums were nose-breeders —the male's penis is forked (one side for each nostril, apparently) and the female grooms her pouch right before giving birth— they assumed she was sneezing the young into the pouch!

TREE SQUIRREL
(to 14 ½ inches)

Depending on your point of view, squirrels may be a bane or a blessing. It's delightful to watch these attractive, inquisitive busybodies eat, groom, and play in a park (which is why Eastern Gray and Eastern Fox Squirrels were introduced to American cities a century ago). It's not so fun when they're noisily galloping over your ceiling, gnawing through wires and insulation, or hogging the seeds from your "squirrel-proof" bird feeder. Persistent problem solvers and acrobatic daredevils, they can leap astounding distances, quickly climb up (and down) almost anything, and even hang from their hind legs using backward-swiveling ankles and sharp claws.

Besides seeds, squirrels eat a little bit of everything: nuts, flowers, fruits, tree buds, mushrooms—and occasionally insects, bird eggs, or nestlings they come across in their travels through the treetops. A squirrel uses a tree cavity or builds a leafy nest in the branches for sleeping at night and raising its young, but accessible attics, chimneys, and wall spaces are convenient substitutes.

Squirrels don't hibernate, so when nuts and seeds are plentiful in late summer and fall, they load up on calories and bury the surplus (often hundreds of nuts), scattering them throughout their territories, sometimes hiding or moving them to make sure they are safe from birds or other squirrels. In the lean days ahead, a squirrel employs its memory and an incredible sense of smell to locate many of the nuts, even if they're buried inches under dirt or snow. Any overlooked nuts sprout into seedlings come spring.

A squirrel communicates with barks, clicks, and clucks (you might think the incessant chatter is a bird unless you follow the sound to its source), and its expressive tail. That same tail balances the squirrel during high-wire acts, and thick, luxurious fur makes for a great blanket, parachute, and umbrella—but it's not so good for helping the squirrel (who can't sweat) to cool down. So on very hot days, a squirrel literally hangs out in the shade, comically draped over a fence or branch, or sprawled flat on the ground.

Urban tree squirrels are a bit difficult to distinguish from one another—Eastern Gray Squirrels are typically gray, but can be brown or black, and have whitish bellies; Eastern Fox Squirrels are usually reddish brown with orange bellies. Western Gray Squirrels, native to the Pacific states, are less urban and have proportionally longer tails.

POCKET GOPHER
(to 8 inches)

Overnight, has your yard been mysteriously polka-dotted with lopsided mounds of soil? Were your pea plants sliced off at ground level or pulled underground altogether? You have a gopher. A connoisseur of roots, shoots, leaves, and bulbs, this little dynamo is made for digging—short, strong legs (with long claws on the front legs), small eyes and ears, and sensitive whiskers for navigation in the dark. Four large, sharp, extra-tough incisors are *outside* the lips, to keep dirt out of its mouth—because the pocket gopher does most of its excavation with its teeth! This allows it to live in harder soils than claw-digging rodents.

A few rodents have cheek pouches they can fill with food for transportation; this gopher has fur-lined "pockets" outside the mouth that can be turned inside out easily to empty the goodies or nesting material.

Pocket gophers are solitary and very territorial, except during breeding season. Each gopher has his or her own system of long, shallow foraging tunnels and deeper (up to six feet) passages with storerooms, nesting areas, and latrines. Openings in the burrow are plugged to keep temperature and humidity constant—if you see an open hole, the resident is probably still digging. Watch for the gopher (whose coat often matches the color of local dirt) bulldozing soil with its head and front legs or peeping out in search of food. They're pretty safe from predators because gophers rarely come out in the open. Sometimes they emerge just far enough to reach plants that grow nearby, but they can pop back in with lightning speed. Hawks, owls, skunks, snakes, coyotes, terriers, and house cats catch gophers if they get a chance.

Gophers are often considered garden and agricultural pests, and there is no end of crazy, questionable contraptions and folk remedies for discouraging them—sonic machines, Juicy Fruit gum, and used cat litter, to name a few. In the natural world, their burrowing activity is a boon—mixing and aerating soil, increasing soil fertility and plant diversity.

HOUSE MOUSE
(to 3 ¼ inches)

True to its name, the House Mouse has been closely associated with humans and our dwellings for at least fifteen thousand years; in fact, archaeologists are using evidence of these mice to help track the transition of ancient humans from roaming hunter-gatherers to sedentary farmers. Originally from Asia, the House Mouse spread to Europe, and then hitched a ride to North America with the waves of colonists. It is the most common mammal on earth, living everywhere people do.

Running up to eight miles per hour, squeezing through spaces just over a quarter inch wide, and able to swim, climb, and jump over a foot high, mice can also sing! When courting (or smelling) a female, a male mouse "sings" surprisingly complex calls that rival some birdsongs, but are too high-pitched for us to hear. Songs may also be used to protect territory.

In the yard, mice eat weed seeds and insects, but in homes or agricultural fields, mice are unwelcome, as they eat and contaminate our food. And they are wildly prolific—a female can breed at about five weeks old, and gestation lasts only three weeks: she can have five to ten litters of young in one year. Wild mice usually live a year or less—they are popular bite-sized meals for any predator quick enough to catch one. It's likely that cats became domesticated by hanging out near the first farms and grain stores, picking off the bountiful rats and mice.

Besides reproducing rapidly, mice are small, cute, easy to keep, and docile—eighteenth-century mouse fanciers bred mice with coat colors, patterns, and textures different from the usual brown, as well as with various behaviors and eye colors.

Scientists took note—lab mice used as models for research on many human disorders and diseases are descendants of the House Mouse.

NORWAY RAT
(to 8 ¾ inches)

Like the House Mouse, the Norway Rat is originally from Asia, is unrelated to its native counterparts, and traveled to the US on the first ships from Europe. Also called the Brown Rat, it was mistakenly given the common name Norway Rat before it had been introduced to Norway! This large rat lives near people on all continents but Antarctica, and it is common near homes, around garbage, and in subway and sewer systems. Intelligent and difficult to catch, and good at climbing, jumping, and running, Norway Rats can cause serious damage to crops, livestock, and buildings. Mostly nocturnal, they dig complex burrows and live in large social groups. Because they are prolific breeders, they are raised for science and medical research, and many people keep them as pets. They're easy to keep, and they are smart, clean, and social, forming close bonds with their owners.

While rats consume most anything, including soap and leather, their primary diet is plant matter, which is notoriously difficult to digest. Some herbivores, like cows, sheep, and deer, have four-chambered stomachs with special bacteria to help break these foods into digestible nutrients, and they "unswallow" their food as cud to re-chew. Rats and mice, with their simple stomachs, have to wait for the food to come out the other end as poop, which they sometimes eat to recover the remaining nutrients.

A rat (or mouse) tail does more than provide balance while climbing—it also helps control body temperature. Unable to sweat, a rat can control circulation through its long, hairless tail, increasing blood flow to release heat in warm weather, or restricting it to retain heat when it's cold.

The Roof Rat is another common introduced rat—smaller and darker, with longer ears and tail than the Norway Rat, it runs across rooftops at night, and nests in trees or attics.

VOLE
(to 5 inches)

A bit larger than mice, with shorter, furred tails and compact, plump, gopher-like bodies, voles (also called meadow mice) are one of the most common mammals in the US—most regions are home to at least one species. Even so, they aren't the most familiar rodents, as they don't invade our homes and they're secretive—a vole lives (often with several others) in a shallow burrow system. Active day and night, they leave the burrow often, but under cover: the burrow's multiple entrances are connected aboveground via a maze of tunnels worn through dense grass or weeds by voles dashing to and fro, eating and collecting plants and seeds. Voles also enjoy roots, tubers, and tree bark—sometimes their enthusiastic chewing kills trees. Voles are as prolific as mice and are related to lemmings; some vole populations go through similar cycles of ebb and flow, occasionally shooting to epic numbers.

MOLE
(to 5 ½ inches)

Moles are digging masters! Specialized for subterranean life, a mole's streamlined, cylindrical body has no external ears to get in the way (or get filled with dirt), and its small, poorly developed eyes are covered with fur since there's not much to see in the dark. They shovel dirt so quickly they nearly swim underground (thanks to muscular shoulders and broad, long-clawed, scooping front paws). A narrow pelvis, flexible spine, and velvety, nondirectional fur allow the mole to easily turn around, back up, or even somersault in the narrow tunnel without getting stuck or being rubbed the wrong way.

Raised ridges across the lawn are shallow feeding tunnels, formed as the mole plows its way through the ground in search of prey. It hunts in the dark using a keen sense of smell and a sensitivity to vibrations in the soil. Each day, a mole can eat close to its own weight in worms, snails, slugs, centipedes, grubs, ants, spiders, and even small mammals. Eastern Moles eat some vegetation, but other moles are not herbivores—the occasional root or bulb nibbled on probably had insect pests inside.

Volcano-like molehills don't have openings because they aren't entrances but rather excess soil from excavation of the second, subterranean tunnel system a mole uses for resting and nesting. Some gardeners find the tunnels and hills unsightly, but they promote drainage, aeration, and rain penetration, and moles eat loads of garden pests.

Plenty of creatures would enjoy mole for dinner, but predation is low because a mole emerges so rarely from the safety of its burrow. In contrast to mice and voles, a mole has a mere single brood of two to five young each year.

NORTHERN RACCOON
(to 24 inches)

This playful, intelligent, and curious masked bandit sleeps during the day in any number of hideouts—a hollow under a tree or rock, beneath a porch, in an abandoned burrow, or up in a tree. At night, the opportunistic omnivore may raid your garbage can, garden shed, or even your home, overturning containers, opening latches, and sorting through cupboards with its nimble fingers, looking for anything edible and leaving an awful mess. If given the opportunity, it prefers to hunt near water for mice, frogs, and shellfish.

Almost two-thirds of a raccoon brain's sensory processing is devoted to its incredibly sensitive hands, so a raccoon can "see" with its hands by picking up and manipulating an item of interest (much as a dog uses its heightened sense of smell for investigation). This ability is particularly useful in the dark or while searching for underwater prey, but is also the raccoon's default mode of exploration. It looks as if the raccoon is washing the object, which has led to a mistaken belief that they are obsessed with cleanliness.

The dark mask probably helps a raccoon identify other individual raccoons, and may help reduce glare (like a football player's eye black), improving night vision.

Raccoon coats were hip in the 1920s, and the bushy, striped tails adorned 1960s Daniel Boone hats. Raccoons are still hunted for sport and because they're considered a nuisance; nonhuman predators include owls and bobcats.

STRIPED SKUNK
(to 20 inches)

The distinctive warning coloration of a Striped Skunk is well known throughout North America. A white line in the middle of the skunk's face splits to form wide stripes along the body and tail. A skunk's anal scent glands are such an effective defense that it doesn't need to hide—it can calmly, confidently rummage in leaf litter and dig in search of insects (including bees and wasps) and the occasional small animal, plant, egg, or morsel of carrion with little worry of being bothered. It would rather not use its precious chemical reserves, so anyone bold enough to pester a skunk is given fair warning: the skunk hisses or growls, stamps its feet, charges, and raises its tail before spraying. Twin jets aim and deliver a mist or streams of liquid (both of which can travel up to twelve feet), causing temporary burning of the eyes and an overwhelmingly noxious scent that lasts and lasts. A concoction of hydrogen peroxide, baking soda, and dishwashing liquid reportedly works better than tomato juice, but the stench is difficult to remove.

Skunks are mainly nocturnal. If you know one is nearby, give it plenty of space and make some noise so it knows you're coming—startling a skunk is a sure-fire way to get sprayed. The greatest perils for skunks are traffic and predatory birds (Great Horned Owls particularly seem to enjoy skunk, like a fine stinky cheese; most other predators steer clear).

Winter is spent mostly in the den, although skunks don't hibernate. Between three and ten playful kits are born in the spring; come summer and early fall, those that survive leave their mother in search of their own territories and dens in rock piles or hollow logs or under houses.

APPENDIX

PLANTS

Anagallis arvensis (Scarlet Pimpernel)
Bellis perennis (Common Daisy)
Erodium cicutarium (Common Storksbill)
Hedera helix (English Ivy)
Hordeum sp. (foxtail)
Malva pseudolavatera (Cretan Mallow)
Matricaria discoidea (Pineappleweed)
Medicago polymorpha (Burclover)
Plantago lanceolata (English Plantain)
Poa pratensis (Kentucky Bluegrass)
Portulaca oleracea (Common Purslane)
Oxalis pes-caprae (Bermuda Buttercup)
Taraxacum officinale (Common Dandelion)
Toxicodendron diversilobum (Western Poison Oak)
Toxicodendron radicans (Eastern Poison Ivy)

ANNELIDS

Eisenia fetida (red wiggler)
Lumbricus rubellus (red wiggler)
Lumbricus terrestris (common earthworm)

MOLLUSKS

Cornu aspersum (Garden Snail)
Deroceras reticulatum (Gray Garden Slug)

ARTHROPODS

Agraulis vanillae (Gulf Fritillary)
Apis mellifera (Honey Bee)
Argiope aurantia (Black and Yellow Garden Spider)
Armadillidium vulgare (pillbug)
Bombus occidentalis (bumble bee)
Ctenocephalides felis (Cat Flea)
Culex pipiens (Common House Mosquito)
Danaus plexippus (Monarch)
Dolichovespula maculata (Bald-Faced Hornet)
Estigmene acraea (woolly bear, Salt Marsh Tiger)
Forficula auricularia (Common Earwig)
Graphocephala atropunctata (leafhopper)
Gryllus pennsylvanicus (Fall Field Cricket)
Hippodamia convergens (Convergent Lady Beetle)
Hylephila phyleus (Fiery Skipper)
Junonia coenia (Buckeye)
Latrodectus hesperus (Western Black Widow)
Linepithema humile (Argentine Ant)
Macrosiphum rosae (Rose Aphid)
Megalographa biloba (inchworm, Bilobed Semilooper)
Melanoplus devastator (Devastating Grasshopper)

Musca domestica (House Fly)
Oxidus gracilis (Greenhouse Millipede)
Papilio rutulus (Western Tiger Swallowtail)
Phalangium opilio (daddy longlegs)
Philaenus spumarius (Meadow Spittlebug)
Pieris rapae (Cabbage White)
Polistes fuscatus (Northern Paper Wasp)
Porcellio scaber (sowbug)
Scudderia furcata (Fork-Tailed Bush Katydid)
Stagmomantis californica (California Mantis)
Stenopelmatus fuscus (Jerusalem Cricket)
Strymon melinus (Gray Hairstreak)
Theatops californiensis (Cryptopid Centipede)
Tipula pubera (crane fly)
Trombidium holosericeum (red velvet mite)
Vanessa annabella (West Coast Lady)
Vespula pensylvanica (Western Yellowjacket)
Xylocopa californica (Carpenter Bee)

AMPHIBIANS

Anaxyrus boreas (Western Toad)
Batrachoseps attenuatus (California Slender Salamander)
Pseudacris regilla (Pacific Treefrog)

REPTILES

Diadophis punctuatus (Ringneck Snake)
Elgaria multicarinata (Southern Alligator Lizard)
Pituophis catenifer (Gopher Snake)
Sceloporus occidentalis (Western Fence Lizard)
Thamnophis elegans (Western Garter Snake)

BIRDS

Aphelocoma californica (California Scrub-Jay)
Calypte anna (Anna's Hummingbird)
Carpodacus mexicanus (House Finch)
Columba livia (Rock Pigeon)
Corvus brachyrhynchos (American Crow)
Corvus corax (Common Raven)
Cyanocitta stelleri (Steller's Jay)
Euphagus cyanocephalus (Brewer's Blackbird)
Junco hyemalis (Dark-Eyed Junco)
Mimus polyglottos (Northern Mockingbird)
Passer domesticus (House Sparrow)
Sternus vulgaris (European Starling)
Turdus migratorius (American Robin)
Zenaida macroura (Mourning Dove)
Zonotrichia leucophrys (White-Crowned Sparrow)

MAMMALS

Didelphis marsupialis (Virginia Opossum)
Mephitis mephitis (Striped Skunk)
Microtus californicus (California Vole)
Mus musculus (House Mouse)
Procyon lotor (Northern Raccoon)
Scapanus latimanus (Broad-Footed Mole)
Sciurus carolinensis (Eastern Gray Squirrel)
Thomomys bottae (Botta's Pocket Gopher)
Rattus norvegicus (Norway Rat)

REFERENCES

Birch, Martin, and Abraham Hefetz. "The Mating of Moths." *New Scientist*, no. 1530 (Oct. 16, 1986): 48–51.

Dunn, Jon L., and Jonathan Alderfer. *Field Guide to the Birds of North America*. 6th ed. Washington, D.C.: National Geographic Society, 2011.

Krause, William J., and Winifred A. Krause. *The Opossum: Its Amazing Story*. Columbia, MO: University of Missouri, 2006.

Powell, Jerry A., and Charles L. Hogue. *California Insects*. Berkeley and Los Angeles: Univ. of California Press, 1979.

Preston-Mafham, Rod, and Ken Preston-Mafham. *The Encyclopedia of Land Invertebrate Behaviour*. Cambridge, MA: MIT Press, 1993.

Shapiro, Arthur M., and Timothy D. Manolis. *Field Guide to Butterflies of the San Francisco Bay and Sacramento Valley Regions*. Berkeley and Los Angeles: Univ. of California Press, 2007.

INTERNET RESOURCES

Agricultural Sustainability Institute. "Earthworm Information." Accessed Sept. 1, 2019. asi.ucdavis.edu/programs/ucsarep/research -initiatives/are/ecosystem/earthworm-information /earthworm-information

Aldaz, Silvia, and Luis M. Escudero. "Imaginal Discs." *Current Biology* 20, no. 10 (2010): R429–R431. DOI:10.1016/j.cub.2010.03.010

Allison, Tara. Welcome Wildlife. Accessed Sept. 1, 2019. welcomewildlife .com

Armstrong, Wayne P. Wayne's Word. Last updated Jan. 1, 2019. www2 .palomar.edu/users/warmstrong

National Audubon Society, The. Audubon. Accessed Sept. 1, 2019. audubon .org

Bay Nature Institute. *Bay Nature.* Accessed Sept. 1, 2019. baynature.org

Bee Culture. *Bee Culture*. Accessed Sept. 1, 2019. beeculture.com

Bee Informed Partnership. Bee Informed. Accessed Sept. 1, 2019. beeinformed.org

Boback, Scott M., Katelyn J. McCann, Kevin A. Wood, Patrick M. McNeal, Emmett L. Blankenship, and Charles F. Zwemer. "Snake Constriction Rapidly Induces Circulatory Arrest in Rats." *Journal of Experimental Biology* 218 (2015): 2279–2288. DOI: 10.1242/jeb.121384

Breene, Robert Gale, III. "Spider Digestion and Food Storage." American Tarantula Society. Accessed Sept. 1, 2019. atshq.org/download /spider-digestion-food-storage

California Academy of Sciences and the National Geographic Society. iNaturalist. Accessed Sept. 1, 2019. inaturalist.org

Cornell Lab of Ornithology, The. "All About Birds." Accessed Sept. 1, 2019. allaboutbirds.org

Davenport, Jason W., and William E. Conner. "Dietary alkaloids and the development of androconial organs in *Estigmene acrea*." *Journal of Insect Science* 3, no. 1 (2003): 3. DOI:10.1093/jis/3.1.3

Eaton, Joe. "Researchers Worry about Worms Worldwide." *Berkeley Daily Planet*, Mar. 4, 2006. berkeleydailyplanet.com /issue/2006-03-14/article/23651

Evangelista, Dennis, Scott Hotton, and Jacques Dumais. "The mechanics of explosive dispersal and self-burial in the seeds of the filaree, *Erodium cicutarium* (Geraniaceae)." *Journal of Experimental Biology* 214 (2011): 521–529. DOI:10.1242/jeb.050567

Fields, Helen. "Why Are Some Feathers Blue?" *Smithsonian Magazine* (Mar. 2012). smithsonianmag.com/science-nature/why-are -some-feathers-blue-100492890

Fumapest Group. "Destructive Termites in California." Termite.com. Accessed Sept. 1, 2019. termite.com/termites/california.html

Gary. "Vintage Men's Socks History." Vintage Dancer. Jan. 12, 2017. vintagedancer.com/vintage/history-vintage-mens-socks

GrrlScientist. "Schemochromes: The Physics of Structural Plumage Colors." *Guardian*, Oct. 16, 2007. theguardian.com /science/punctuated-equilibrium/2007/oct/16/birds-physics

Hadley, Debbie. "10 Fascinating Facts about Ladybugs." ThoughtCo. Last updated July 12, 2019. thoughtco.com/fascinating-facts-about -ladybugs-1968120

Holy, Timothy E., Zhongsheng Guo. "Ultrasonic Songs of Male Mice." *PLOS Biology* 3, no.12 (Nov. 1, 2005): e386. DOI:10.1371

/journal.pbio.0030386

How Stuff Works. "Animals." Accessed Sept. 1, 2019. animals.howstuffworks
.com

Iowa State University, Department of Entomology. Bug Guide. Accessed
Sept. 1, 2019. bugguide.net

Kasprak, Alex, and David Mikkelson. "Does a Female Praying Mantis
Always Eat Her Mate's Head?" Critter Country, Snopes, Oct. 31,
1999. snopes.com/critters/wild/mantis1.asp

Lavoipierre, Frederique. "Garden Allies: Earthworms." *Pacific Horticulture* 70,
no. 1 (2009). pacifichorticulture.org/articles/earthworms

Lawn Institute, The. "Lawns and Lawn History." Accessed Sept. 1, 2019.
thelawninstitute.org/pages/education/lawn-history/lawns-and
-lawn-history

Liang, Alan Y., and Brian Y. Liang. Liang Insects. Accessed Sept. 1, 2019.
lianginsects.com

Lindsey, Kieran J. Next-Door Nature. Accessed Sept. 1, 2019.
nextdoornature.org

Lotts, Kelly, and Thomas Naberhaus, coordinators. Butterflies and Moths of
North America. Accessed Sept. 1, 2019. butterfliesandmoths.org

Max Planck Society. "Wild Wheat Shows Its Muscles." May 10, 2007.
mpg.de/551648/pressrelease20070510

Melzer, Björn, Tina Steinbrecher, Robin Seidel, Oliver Kraft, Ruth
Schwaiger, and Thomas Speck. "The Attachment Strategy of
English Ivy." *Journal of The Royal Society Interface* 7, no. 50 (May 12,
2010): e20100140. DOI:10.1098/rsif.2010.0140

Mid-Atlantic Apiculture Research and Extension Consortium (MAAREC).
"Honey Bee Biology." Accessed Sept. 1, 2019. agdev.anr.udel.edu
/maarec/honey-bee-biology

Mihir and Ameet. "Insects of San Francisco Bay Area." San Francisco Bay
Area Wildlife. Accessed Sept. 1, 2019. sfbaywildlife.info/species
/insects.htm#grasshoppers

Muth, Felicity. "How to Find the Perfect Female if You're a Black Widow
Spider." Not Bad Science (blog), *Scientific American,* June 29, 2011.
blogs.scientificamerican.com/not-bad-science/how-to-find-the
-perfect-female-if-you-8217-re-a-black-widow-spider

Nafis, Gary. California Herps—A Guide to the Amphibians and Reptiles of
California. Accessed Sept. 1, 2019. californiaherps.com

Ostovar, Vicky. "Drosophila: High Resolution Imaging of Imaginal Disc Development." Developmental Biology Interactive. Accessed Sept. 1, 2019. www.devbio.biology.gatech.edu/?page_id=367

Planet Natural. "Lawn History." Planet Natural Research Center. Accessed Sept 1, 2019. planetnatural.com/organic-lawn-care-101/history/

Price, Michael. "When Did Humans Settle Down? The House Mouse May Have Have the Answer." *Science,* Mar. 27, 2017. sciencemag.org /news/2017/03/when-did-humans-settle-down-house-mouse -may-have-answer

Regents of the University of California, The. University of California Agriculture and Natural Resources. Accessed Sept. 1, 2019. ucanr.edu

Reise, Heike. "A review of mating behavior in slugs of the genus Deroceras (Pulmonata: Agriolimacidae)." *American Malacological Bulletin* 23, no. 1 (2007): 137–156. DOI:10.4003/0740-2783-23.1.137

Roach, John, "Froghopper Bug Crowned 'World's Greatest Leaper." National Geographic News. *National Geographic.* (July 30, 2003) byjohnroach.com/writings/blog/froghopper-bug-crowned -worlds-greatest-leaper.html

Sanchez-Arroyo, Hussein, and John L. Capinera. "House Fly." Featured Creatures. University of Florida, Entomology and Nematology Department. Last revision 2017. entnemdept.ufl.edu/creatures /urban/flies/house_fly.htm

Shapiro, Art. Art Shapiro's Butterfly Site. Accessed Sept. 1, 2019. butterfly.ucdavis.edu

Sibley, David. "What the Changing Colors of a Songbird's Bill Mean." *David Sibley's ID Toolkit* (blog), *Bird Watching.* Accessed Aug. 1, 2017. birdwatchingdaily.com/blog/2015/06/11/david-sibley -what-the-changing-colors-of-a-songbirds-bill-mean

Skilbeck, Christopher "Bot." "Insect Antennae." Cronodon. Accessed Sept. 1, 2019. cronodon.com/BioTech/Insects_antenna.html

Smith, Elizabeth Zimmerman. Sialis. Accessed Sept. 1, 2019. sialis.org

Stiles, Gary F. "Aggressive and Courtship Displays of the Male Anna's Hummingbird." *The Condor* 84, no. 2 (1982): 208–225. DOI:10.2307/1367674

Strange, Carolyn J. "Botta's Pocket Gopher or Valley Pocket Gopher." Friends of Edgewood. Accessed Sept. 1, 2019. friendsofedgewood.org/gopher

U.S. Department of Agriculture. Agricultural Research Service. Accessed
    Sept. 1, 2019. ars.usda.gov

University of California, Riverside. Center for Invasive Species Research.
    Accessed Sept. 1, 2019. cisr.ucr.edu

VanEngelsdorp, Dennis, and Marina Doris Meixner. "A historical review of
    managed honey bee populations in Europe and the United States
    and the factors that may affect them." Supplement, *Journal of
    Invertebrate Pathology* 103 (2010): S80–S95. DOI:10.1016
    /j.jip.2009.06.011

Vincent, Morgan. "*Forficula auricularia:* European earwig." Animal Diversity
    Web. Accessed Sept. 1, 2019. animaldiversity.org/accounts
    /Forficula_auricularia

Walker, Thomas J., ed. "Genus *Gryllus*: Field Crickets." Singing Insects of
    North America (SINA). Accessed Sept. 1, 2019. entnemdept.ufl
    .edu/walker/buzz/g464a.htm

Wildscreen. "Common European Earwig (*Forficula auriculeria*)."
    web.archive.org/web/20190105021636/arkive.org
    /common-european-earwig/forficula-auricularia

Yong, Ed. "3-D Scans Reveal Caterpillars Turning into Butterflies." Not
    Exactly Rocket Science (blog), *National Geographic*, May 14,
    2013. nationalgeographic.com/science/phenomena
    /2013/05/14/3-d-scans-caterpillars-transforming-butterflies
    -metamorphosis

ABOUT THE AUTHOR

Marni Fylling has been enchanted by the natural world for as long as she can remember, finding her earliest inspirations in her urban backyard and her dad's college biology textbook. She has a B.S. in zoology from UC Davis and a graduate certificate in natural science illustration from UC Santa Cruz. A science illustrator, writer, and educator, her favorite activity is exploring tide pools, although sketching insects and wildflowers (or just about anything else) is a close second.

Photo Credit: Song Nelson